THE
LEADERSHIP
PAPERS

St Matthias Press

Contents

The Programme

One of the essential characteristics of the Christian leader is a firm grasp of sound doctrine. As Paul says to Titus: "He [the elder] must hold firmly to the trustworthy message as it has been taught, so that he can encourage others by sound doctrine and refute those who oppose it". Without a thorough knowledge of the Bible's teaching in the important and fundamental areas, our decision-making and leadership will be seriously disadvantaged and ultimately flawed.

The series of papers that make up this training programme are designed to provoke thought and discussion around these fundamental truths of Christianity. There are nine papers (plus an introduction and appendix) each one based on a statement in the Doctrinal Basis of the Australian Fellowship of Evangelical Students (AFES). These statements (with some minor regional variations) are used throughout Australia as the doctrinal standard of Evangelical student groups. (With only minor differences, this is also the Doctrinal Basis of Scripture Union and the Crusader Union). Together , these nine doctrinal statements form a clear and very helpful summary of what Evangelical Christianity believes — they deserve careful study and thought.

The papers are best read with an open Bible close to hand, both to look up the footnotes and to do the Bible research sections that are interspersed throughout. The **Think it Through** questions that follow each paper are designed for personal reflection and then discussion. Make sure you discuss your thoughts with someone before proceeding to the next paper, whether a friend, or your minister or Bible study leader, or your local student staffworker.

Bibliography

There are a number of helpful books that are worth consulting in your study of basic doctrines of Christianty. The best are:

In Understanding Be Men by T C Hammond (IVP)
Know the Truth by Bruce Milne (IVP)
Systematic Theology by Louis Berkhof (Banner of Truth)
God's Words by J I Packer (Hodder & Stoughton)
The New Bible Dictionary (Hodder & Stoughton)

Consult the tables of contents and indexes in these books to find articles, scripture references and detailed bibliographies on the subjects discussed in these papers.

What is Evangelicalism?

Who wants to be an 'ism'?

Most of us do not like the idea We do not want to be labelled, or pigeon-holed, or lumped in with a particular party or movement.

However, 'isms' are a necessary evil of normal human interaction. Most of us represent particular traditions or viewpoints and we *can* be analysed as groups, as well as individuals.

Certainly, in our Christianity, we should respond to God personally, not from social pressure or tradition. However, if the gospel calls for a particular, specific response, then all who profess the name of Jesus should be able to be grouped together. They should be able to be defined as an 'ism'. Perhaps 'Christianism'.

Unfortunately, 'Christianism' suffers from major disagreements. Some people understand the gospel in one way; others flatly contradict that understanding; and each wishes to call their own understanding of the gospel 'genuine Christianity'. While we may all want to call ourselves 'Christian', there will arise other labels to differentiate what kind of Christian is being meant. 'Genuine Christian' as opposed to 'spurious Christian' is hardly adequate. 'Protestant Christian', 'Orthodox Christian', 'Catholic Christian', 'Liberal', 'Charismatic', 'Reformed', 'Presbyterian', 'Baptist': the list seems endless. 'Evangelicalism' is one of these terms.

The Background

Evangelicalism is a very ancient concept. The word 'evangelical' comes from the Greek word meaning 'gospel'. In English it is commonly an adjective meaning one who *believes* the gospel; an 'evangel-ist' is one who *preaches* the gospel. In that sense, all Christians would want to claim to be Evangelicals and all Evangelicals would want to claim to be evangelists. It is easy to understand how confusion about the term can creep in.

However, historically the term has had particular coinage at different points. During the Reformation, on the continent, the Lutherans in particular were called Evangelicals. Frequently to this day, Protestants do not go by the name 'Protestant' but by the term 'Evangelical'. However, in England the term gained greater usage during the 'Evangelical Awakening' at the end of the 18th century through the preaching of George Whitefield, John and Charles Wesley and others. At that stage, the term was loved by those who were Evangelicals and formed part of the abuse levelled by outsiders. The recovery of the gospel message during the Reformation and the Evangelical Awakening, made the term 'Evangelical' particularly appropriate to these groups.

During the 20th century, the term 'Evangelical' has grown in acceptance, respectability and popularity. The Evangelical movement has grown steadily in most Protestant churches. Evangelical churches have grown in numbers and this, together with the decline in non-evangelical and anti-evangelical churches, has lead many people to jump on the bandwagon and call themselves 'Evangelical'.

Furthermore, the desire of Evangelicals to gain greater intellectual, ecclesiastical, and political credibility within the Christian community has lead to a broader definition of the term. Consequently, just as most modern Protestants do not know what they are protesting about, so most Evangelicals are losing touch with the evangel.

Gone are the days when people of different theological positions attacked Evangelicals as being narrow-minded or extreme. Now much more commonly, we find people claiming to **be** Evangelicals and then redefining the word in their own terms, changing its essentials so as to render it unrecognisable. This approach to Evangelicalism has had a very much more profound impact than the persecution of previous generations. Seduction from within has sullied the once pure grasp Evangelicals had of the gospel.

The Definition: Theological Experience

Given this background, should we attempt to define Evangelicalism in terms of its history? It always was a movement, full of diversity, rather than a precisely defined organisation. Wesley and Whitefield disagreed theologically. Baptists and Brethren disagreed with Anglicans and Presbyterians over issues such as baptism or church membership.

However, the touchstone of Evangelicalism has never been a set of traditions or a particular heritage. The distinguishing feature of an Evangelical has always been a particular under-standing of the gospel—an understanding that is lived out in daily discipleship.

In other words, *Evangelicalism is a theology of experience.* Evangelicals maintain that the gospel calls upon people to repent and put their faith in God. They claim to have been reborn by the Spirit of God so that they know him as their Father and Christ as their Lord. It is more than just believing a series of propositions. It is basing your life upon the great truths of the gospel.

This has confused some people who think that anyone who experiences what they would call 'God' must therefore be an Evangelical. But Evangelical experience of God is a theologi-cally defined and described experience of God. It is experienc-ing God through the 'evangel'. Evangelicalism can be defined, then, in terms of a theological understanding of the gospel, provided we remember that this understanding of the gospel involves our everyday life experience.

We may have reached a stage where the word 'evangelical' is no longer specific enough to be of any use. Perhaps those of us who have been Evangelicals need to devise a new word to describe our particular 'ism'. However, many of the great societies, set up by our forefathers, have this word 'evangelical' in their constitutions. To lose touch with this word would be to lose touch with this history and our institutions. Furthermore, no other word has arisen that rightly describes what we stand for. We need to remind ourselves of the theological understand-ing of the term 'evangelical' and to fight for our exclusive right to use it.

Single Issue Descriptions

It is possible to describe the theology of Evangelicalism in different ways. One hallmark of Evangelicalism has been the doctrine of the **assurance of salvation**. This litmus test has been very useful in the past. It is only those who believe in the substitutionary death of Jesus, promising certain rescue from the wrath to come, who hold to assurance of salvation. Those who believe in morality, always doubt their performance and therefore their assurance of salvation. This issue has the further advantage of taking us into the realm of life experience, rather than being simply a dry, doctrinal statement. However, with the ever increasing trend towards Universalism, many people are assured of their salvation on the wrong basis! Furthermore, a growing number of non-Evangelicals have been persuaded of the truth of this part of Evangelical belief, while still denying other important gospel truths.

Other single issue definitions of Evangelicalism have been proposed. The split between Evangelicals and Liberals at the beginning of this century, was over **the centrality of the atoning work of Christ.** The substitutionary nature of the death of Jesus gave many Evangelicals no choice but to proclaim the cross as fundamental to gospel understanding and essential in its proclamation. However, again it may be argued that many non-Evangelicals retain the doctrine of the substitutionary work of Christ. It is problematic whether this continues to occupy the central place in their faith and evangelism, but in theory they would say it does.

Likewise some people put forward the issue of **the authority of the Scriptures** as the hallmark of Evangelicalism. It is true that Evangelicals are committed to the authority of Scripture. It is also true that other theological positions have a different base of authority. Yet this pushes Evangelicalism slightly away from the gospel itself. Hearing and obeying the word of God is a gospel issue, but is not *the gospel.*

It is best to return to a fuller theological statement to understand the nature of Evangelicalism. Such a statement can be found in the doctrinal basis of the Australian Fellowship of Evangelical Students (AFES). The AFES is a fellowship of Evangelical student groups from around Australia, committed to evangelism and ministry in our tertiary institutions. All office bearers in groups affiliated with the Fellowship are required to sign this basis (or one very similar to it) before taking responsibility for leadership of student groups. The AFES Doctrinal Basis is also used by Scripture Union (with two minor variations) as its standard of belief, and beach mission members and others involved with SU are supposed to be in agreement with these fundamentals of Evangelicalism. This Doctrinal Basis is a very helpful one, for it sets out the fundamentals of Christian belief in a fashion which is both gospel-centred and carefully exclusive of common 20th century heresies. It reads:

A   The divine inspiration and infallibility of Holy Scripture, as originally given, and its supreme authority in all matters of faith and conduct

B   The unity of the Father, the Son and the Holy Spirit in the Godhead

C   The universal sinfulness and guilt of human nature since the fall, rendering man subject to God's wrath and condemnation

D   The conception of Jesus Christ by the Holy Spirit and his birth of the virgin Mary

E   Redemption from the guilt, penalty and power of sin, only through the sacrificial death, as our representative and substitute, of Jesus Christ, the incarnate Son of God

F   The bodily resurrection of Jesus Christ from the dead

G   The necessity of the work of the Holy Spirit to make the death of Christ effective in the individual sinner, granting him repentance toward God and faith in Jesus Christ

H   The indwelling and work of the Holy Spirit in the believer

I   The expectation of the personal return of the Lord Jesus Christ

In subsequent study papers, we will look at these doctrinal statements in order to sharpen our understanding of 'sound doctrine', and pursue the implications for our witness and work in the world.

Note

The Scripture Union Doctrinal Basis does not include Article D on the virgin birth, and adds a statement on the church: "The one, holy, universal Church which is the body of Christ and to which all true believers belong".

Think it Through

1   Is Evangelicalism basically an experience of God or a theological viewpoint?

2   Why do we need to have a doctrinal statement of our beliefs? Wouldn't it be sufficient 'just to believe the Bible'?

3   Would you describe yourself as an 'Evangelical'? If so, why? If not, why not?

Circles and Tangents

The Bible has always been a battleground for Christians, both from without and within. Those who reject Christianity rightly see the Bible as their point of attack. Amongst those who profess to be Christians (but are not) we also find sustained attacks upon the Scriptures. The traditional divisions between the denominations are often divisions of attitudes towards the Bible.

Because the Scriptures are the supreme authority in all matters of faith and conduct, disagreements at this point lead to much wider disputes on a whole range of subjects. Those who take the Bible as the authoritative norm of life will obviously have different views from those who take other books, prophets or experiences as their standard. And there can be little hope of reconciliation when people disagree upon the basic supreme authority.

Most groups use the Bible. But using the Bible is not the same as believing the Bible. The Mormons frequently quote the Bible on our doorsteps yet believe that the Bible is full of errors. Roman Catholicism reads parts of the Bible in the Mass, yet sees the authority for faith and life as found in the traditions of Christ, only part of which is the Bible. Many Liberal Protestant preachers will refer to the Bible, and when the Bible agrees with them will quote it with authority, but in fact they sit in judgement over the Bible, thinking their own wisdom wiser than the wisdom of God. To trust in the Bible as the supreme authority in all matters of faith and conduct, requires one neither to add nor subtract from it. Using the Bible is very different from believing the Bible.

The Evangelical Position on Scripture

The first statement of the AFES doctrinal basis is:

The divine inspiration and infallibility of Holy Scripture, as originally given, and its supreme authority in all matters of faith and conduct.

This is frequently seen as **the** distinctive of evangelical belief. It certainly does mark Evangelicals out from the crowd. However, it is only part of the matrix of truths found in the doctrinal basis of Evangelicalism. Without a belief in the personal, sovereign God, the doctrine of Scripture would not stand. Similarly, without the doctrine of Scripture we would not come to know the personal, sovereign God.

Clarifying Terms

The statement of the AFES doctrinal basis uses clearly recognisable doctrinal jargon to express with accuracy its viewpoint. It is important that we master this jargon in order to avoid misunderstandings.

1. The Divine Inspiration

This refers to the inspiration of the Scriptures by God. The use of the word 'inspiration' comes from 2 Timothy 3:16 and refers to God "breathing out" the Scriptures. It means more than the Scriptures are 'inspired', or that they 'inspire' us. Shakespeare, Mozart and Rembrandt could all be described as 'inspired', by which we mean 'way above average'. They may also have an 'inspiring' effect upon us, by which we mean 'they lift us out of our normal, mundane lives'. However, theologically and Biblically, the idea of inspiration is that the words are breathed out by God—the words of Scripture are God's words.

This in no way implies the **method** by which God inspires. It does not commit us to any idea of mechanical dictation or automatic writing. The inspiration did not remove the personality or style of the human author. The Scriptures are treated as if there is a dual authorship: God and man, with the primary author being God. Psalm 110:1 is said to have been written by David[1] and by God[2] and by David speaking by the Spirit[3]. This dual authorship can be seen throughout the Scriptures[4].

[1] Acts 2:34,35
[2] Heb 1:13
[3] Matt 22:43-44
[4] cf Acts 3:7-11; Heb 4:3-8; Acts 3:22; 4:25

2. Infallibility

The Scriptures can be relied upon completely. They will never fail us—this is what is meant by the traditional term 'infallible'. The Bible is completely trustworthy because its author has made sure that it is without error.

At this point some Evangelical Christians have differed with others by trying to claim too much for the infallibility of Scripture. The Bible is unique and can only be described, never defined. To say that it is infallible is a description of its character, not a definition by which we can determine the ways in which God is going to speak. Thus some parts of the Bible (the parables, for example) may be fiction and yet still be described as infallible. Other parts of the Scriptures may involve poetic licence and exaggeration, without losing their veracity[1]. While on one hand we must be wary of doubting the absolute trustworthiness and truthfulness of the Scriptures, on the other hand we must not claim too much for the Scriptures, thus squeezing them into an unbiblical strait-jacket. Infallible history must have incidental variations in the reporting of events, otherwise it is not history at all. Such minor variations do not effect the Scripture's infallibility.

[1] Note, for example, Jesus' striking language in Luke 14:26

'Holy Scripture' refers to the whole Bible comprising the old and new covenants. These 66 books are the written words of God. However, the version that has been inspired and is entirely trustworthy is the original version. Not every copy or translation of the Bible is the divine, inspired, infallible word of God. God gave his revelation to mankind through his authors. On different occasions, mankind in his neglect and sinfulness has tampered with and varied what was originally given.

3. Holy Scripture as Originally Given

Fortunately, none of the original copies have been kept, otherwise we would be tempted to venerate and worship them. However, it is important for us to study carefully the manuscripts that are available, to ascertain the original message of God. In God's great kindness, many thousands of copies of the Scriptures have been preserved, along with considerable knowledge of the means by which they have been transmitted to us. Thus we can be assured that what we have today is substantially what was originally given. The variations between manuscripts are so small that no doctrine can be said to hang on them.

The phrase 'supreme authority' indicates that the doctrinal basis acknowledges the existence of other authorities. This is because the Scriptures themselves recognise other authorities. Governments are put in authority over people just as fathers are put in authority over children. However, the supreme authority, the authority over all other authorities[2], is said to be Scripture. There is no authority equal to, or over, the Scriptures.

4. Supreme Authority

[2] Rom 13:1; 1 Pet 2:13

Notice too that the authority of Scripture is limited to matters of faith and conduct. The Scriptures do not claim to be an authority in calculus, nuclear physics, poetry or chess. There may be some aspects of these disciplines where the Scriptures have some relevance, but by and large, these topics are not ad-

5. Faith and Conduct

dressed, and there is no claim to supreme authority here.

Rather, the Scriptures are God-breathed and useful for "teaching, rebuking, correcting and training in righteousness, so that the man of God may be thoroughly equipped for every good work"[1]. It is in the area of faith and conduct that the Scriptures are speaking. 'Faith' refers to more than our trust in God; it includes the idea of **the** faith that was delivered once and for all to the saints.[2]

[1] 2 Tim 3:16-17

[2] Jude 3

Why does the Bible have authority?

God is personal and revelatory. He reveals himself to be living and speaking and truthful. He is the sovereign Lord of the universe who rules the world by his word and reveals himself in his speech. What has this to do with the Bible's authority?

1 God's Character

The Thessalonians turned from idols to serve the "living and true God"[3] This is characteristic of the description of God in the Scriptures. Psalm 115 points to God as being radically different from the idols who "have mouths, but cannot speak". Jeremiah scorns the following of such idols; he says, "Like a scarecrow in a melon patch, their idols cannot speak, they must be carried because they cannot walk"[4]. The God of Israel, on the other hand, speaks: "By the word of the Lord were the heavens made, their starry host by the breath of his mouth...for he spoke, and it came to be; he commanded, and it stood firm". [5]

[3] Thess 1:9

[4] Jer 10:5

[5] Ps 33:6,9; Isa 44-45

However, God not only speaks; he speaks the **truth**. The "true and living God" is not only true in that he really exists, but is also true in his character and nature. Two of the things which are said to be impossible for God are telling lies[6] and disowning himself.[7] God is faithful to his word and consequently, God's word is right and true.[8] It is on this basis that we affirm that the Holy Scriptures are infallible.

[6] Heb 6:18

[7] 2 Tim 2:13

[8] Heb 10:33; Ps 33:4; Ps 119:142,151

2 Ruling, Revealing, Relating

God rules his universe by his word. By his powerful word he created the world[9] and by the same word he will destroy it.[10] God's word always achieves his purpose[11]—it is living and active, penetrating and judging.[12] So much is the word of God an expression of God himself and of his powerful rule in this world, that the **word** of God can be used to explain the incarnation. [13]

[9] Gen 1; Ps 33:6

[10] 2 Pet 3:7

[11] Isa 55:11

[12] Heb 4:12-13

[13] Jn 1:1-8

[14] Heb 1:1-3

However, the word of God not only rules the world, but also reveals God to the world. In the past God spoke through the prophets, but in these last days he has spoken to us by his Son.[14] The word of truth, the gospel of salvation, has been spoken to us to reveal the great plan of God in redemption.[1] Even to the Gentiles the unsearchable riches of Christ have been made plain[2].

[1]Eph 1:13
[2]Eph 3:1-13

God relates to us through this revelation. He makes himself known by it, and through it he regenerates us. The preaching of Jesus Christ as Lord is used by God to give us the knowledge of the glory of God in the face of Christ.[3] The gospel is the power of God for salvation for everyone who believes.[4] By the message of the cross we come to know the power of God and the wisdom of God and God himself.[5]

[3]2 Cor 4:5-6
[4]Romans 1:16

[5]1 Cor 1

Thus, the reason that the Bible has authority is because of its author—God. The sovereign Lord of heaven and earth has spoken through the prophets and in his Son. To reject the word of God is to reject God himself.

What Authority has the Bible?

The Scripture has authority over all matters on which it speaks. It is not exhaustive—it does not cover all matters—but because of its authorship its authority extends over everything it covers.

The Bible is not imprisoned in a particular historical context. It was delivered at a point, or more accurately a phase, of history and to understand it correctly we need to read it in its original context. However, the Bible is a contemporary word which does not need to be 'made relevant'. It is permanently relevant because God is speaking his word to **us**.

1 Contemporary

Jesus attacked the Sadducees for ignorance of the Scriptures saying, "Have you not read what God said to **you**".[6] A similar argument is used in Hebrews 3 and 4, where the temptation in the wilderness speaks a word of God to us **today**. In fact, referring to the Exodus, Paul goes so far as to say that "those things happened to them as examples and were written down as warnings for us, on whom the fulfilment of the ages has come"[7].

[6]Matt 22:31

[7]1Cor 10:11; cf Rom 15:4

It is important to understand that the Scriptures are sufficient for Christian living. God's revelation of himself is not partial, but final. In the past it was a partial revelation, when he "spoke through the prophets in many and various ways"[8]. In the past, angels as well as prophets wondered what they were speaking about when they spoke of the salvation that was to come and predicted the sufferings of the Christ. In the gospel these things have now been completely revealed.[9]

2 Sufficient

[8]Heb 1:1

[9]1 Pet 1:10-12

Christ opened the minds of his disciples to understand that

Rev 1:2-3; Rev 19:10

he had come to fulfil the Scriptures by his suffering and resurrection.[1] He brings the Scriptures to their close[2]. All the prophets find their "yes and amen" in him. Now the spirit of prophecy is the testimony of Jesus.[3]

Research

Look up the following verses and see what they reveal about the place of God's word in the Christian life.

Acts 20:32

Romans 15:14

1 Corinthians 2:12-16 (cf. 1 John 2:27)

2 Timothy 3:16-17

Jude 3 (cf. 2 Timothy 1:13-14; 2:2)

How do we Know?

The arguments so far seem to be circular. The Bible claims that the Bible is authoritative. If you believe the Bible, you will believe that it is authoritative.

What happens if you don't believe the Bible? How can you ever get onto the circle? What happens if you believe the book of Mormon, or the Koran? These books also claim to be the authoritative word of God. Their authority seems every bit as circular as the Bible's.

On one level, we should expect that the authority of the Bible will be found within the Bible itself. If it were found elsewhere, then there would be a rival claim to authority in matters of faith and conduct. If, for example, it was by reason that we concluded that the Scriptures were authoritative, then reason would become the supreme authority. The question remains: How can we ever get onto the circle?

1 The Work of the Holy Spirit Why do we believe in Scripture? Because of God's Spirit at work in us. It is God who opens our eyes to see the glory of God

18

in the face of Christ[1]. Paul thanked **God** that the Thessalonians received the word of Paul not as the word of man, but as the word of God[2]. It is because we are his sheep that we know the voice of Jesus[3]. In other words, the Scriptures are Spirit-authenticated

[1] 2 Cor 4:5-6

[2] 1 Thess 2:13

[3] John 10:27

The converse is also true. Those who reject the authority of the Bible usually wish to do so on 'rational' grounds. Their intellect cannot stomach what they read (to mix metaphors). We need to remember, however, that the decision to reject God is fundamentally spiritual, not rational. The man who says in his heart "There is no God" is a fool, not a member of the intelligentsia.[4]

[4] Ps 14:1; cf 1Cor 2:14

2 The Example of Christ

If we are to be followers of Christ, then we should imitate Christ's attitude to the Scriptures. Jesus consistently quoted and referred to the Scriptures as having authority. He considered the Old Testament as a 'court of final appeal' in matters of controversy.[5] He insisted that prophecy would find its fulfilment in his actions.[6] He attacked the Sadducees for their failure to know the Scriptures.[7]

[5] Matt 22:29-32; Mk 7:6-13

[6] Matt 26:52-56

[7] Mark 12:23

[8] 2Tim 3:16; Heb 3-4; 2Pet 1:21; 1 Cor 10:6-11.

As if this wasn't enough, the rest of the New Testament demonstrates the same acceptance of the authority of Scripture.[8] The New Testament even quotes itself as having such authority.[9]

[9] 1Tim 5:18; 2Pet 3: 15-17; 1 Cor 7:40; 14:36-37

3 The Reasonableness of Belief

If we are Christians, and have the Holy Spirit within us and are seeking to follow the example of Christ and his apostles, it can be seen that accepting the authority of the Scriptures is thoroughly reasonable. In fact, denial of the Scriptures is a genuine symptom of unbelief. But what of those outside of Christ? Can this reasonableness ever be demonstrated to them?

The reasonableness of belief can certainly be demonstrated, if not proven. If the Scriptures are true, they must be consistent with what we know of the world. If there was a major inconsistency between our knowledge of the world and our knowledge in Scripture, then it would be hard for people ever to climb onto the circle of belief. Another way of saying this is that the circle of belief touches on the world that we know. These points of contact are like tangents onto the circle. One chief point of contact is history.

We cannot *prove* the truth of the gospel through history. However, history can help us onto the circle. From a purely historical standpoint, we can learn something of the person of Jesus, who he claimed to be and whether those claims measure up to the facts as we have them. This knowledge may lead us to think seriously about his claims over our lives and the meaning he gives to our existence. Such an approach can lead us to accept that belief in Jesus is quite 'reasonable'.

The same point can be made negatively. The Bible speaks about the nature of the world and humanity. Its perception of man as being universally sinful is a reasonable assessment of the state of the world. If it was unreasonable it would be hard to commend to outsiders.

It is at this point that the controversy between science and revelation begins. Is the Bible's view of the world 'unreasonable' in the light of our empirical knowledge? It would be hard to maintain belief in the Scriptures if it taught authoritatively that the world was flat or that the moon was a crescent. However, the description of man and the world in the Scriptures is sufficiently consistent with our empirical knowledge of the world for there to be no real conflict.

These tangents onto the circle of faith have limited apologetic and evangelistic usefulness. They must not be given authority over the Scriptures. Nor must they be seen as an alternative to hearing the Scriptures read and taught, for faith comes from hearing the word of God[1]. It is the gospel word which is the power of God for salvation[2]. It is the miracle of God's Spirit regenerating us through his word that enables people to come to faith in the gospel.

[1] Rom 10:17
[2] Rom 1:16

The Correct Response to Scripture

[3] Exodus 19:16
[4] Psalm 111:10

When the people of God gathered around Mt Sinai, they heard the voice of God and they trembled[3]. In the presence of God man is afraid, and this fear is the beginning of wisdom[4]. The appropriate response to the word of God is the same as our response to God himself.

[5] Like the Bereans of Acts 17.

[6] Deut 6:4-8
[7] Joshua 1:8

We must not merely be hearers of the word, but doers, humbly accepting what God says and earnestly seeking by his strength to put it into operation. We must be people who search out what God is saying[5]. God calls upon us to have his word on our hearts and in our minds, as we get up in the morning and go to bed at night, as we go in and out of our house, and as we teach our children[6]. We are to meditate (that is, to think not to 'mystically meditate') upon his word day and night[7].

[8] Matt 4:4; Deut 8:3

If we have God's word, then we have life, for "man does not live by bread alone but by every word that proceeds from the mouth of God"[8].

Think it Through

1 Is the authority of Scripture being undermined in your own situation? Are there ways in which it is being 'used' rather than 'believed'? What might you do about it?

2 Does God still speak today? If so, how?

3 How will the doctrine of Scripture affect the way in which we minister?

Other Notes

2

What makes Christians Different

In the market bazaar of modern thought, there are many things that make Christianity distinctive. The doctrine of the Trinity is one of these distinctives. The Trinity is a uniquely Christian idea, distinguishing us from all other philosophical and religious systems, as well as differentiating genuine and spurious Christianity.

It may be possible to arrive at monotheism from reflecting on our experience of life. In many cultures around the world, people have believed in the existence of one ultimate God, and this is hardly surprising, since the Bible tells us that God reveals his existence and power through the created order.

However, the knowledge that this One God is at the same time three persons, can come only through the revelation of Scripture. The One God is not a simple unity, but a complex unity of Father, Son and Spirit. We could never conceive of such a thing, except by God revealing it to us in his word.

The first of the statements of the AFES doctrinal basis affirms this doctrine of the Trinity:

> *The Unity of the Father, the Son and the Holy Spirit*
> *in the Godhead.*

What are we to make of this mathematically unusual idea? If the word 'trinity' is not in the Bible, is it necessary for Christians to believe this doctrine? Is it very important anyway?

A Complex Unity

Both the Old and New Testaments are adamant that God is one. God declares that he, Yahweh, is the one Lord of all the earth—there is no other God but him[1]. The worship of other beings and creatures is therefore condemned in the Scriptures. God will not share his glory with images or idols, whether of

[1] Isaiah 45 contains several examples of this.

himself or anything else. Israel, to whom he had revealed himself, was to worship no-one and nothing else, for God is a jealous God who will not share his glory with another. A Christian is one who turns from idols to serve the true and living God[1].

Even the one who is referred to as "the god of this world" is not to be considered in anyway God's equal. There may be angels and principalities and powers, but all of them have been created and are under the sovereign control of the one true God.

Yet, this one God is not a simple, but a complex unity.

In the Old Testament

Within the Old Testament, there are several indications of this complexity. Taken by themselves, these indications would not be sufficient for us to understand the doctrine of the Trinity. However, given the way the New Testament develops the idea, these Old Testament indications of the complex unity of the Godhead can be understood.

A phrase such as "Let us make man in our own image", could be understood as a royal plural if not for the New Testament[2]. However, the New Testament makes clear that all things were made by and for the Son—the Father and the Son were together involved in creation. Genesis 1:26 reveals a God who is Father, Son and Holy Spirit; a God who makes man in his own complex image[3].

Other indications of the complex unity of God are given in passages where the Spirit of God, or the angel of the LORD, or the word of God, or the wisdom of God, seem to be acting as separate from God and yet **being** God at the same time[4].

Sometimes the Old Testament prophesies the coming of the Messiah in terms of divinity. In Isaiah 9:6, the name of the promised child is to be 'Mighty God.' Or in Psalm 45:6-7, God sets someone who is called 'God ' above his companions.

In the New Testament

However, with the coming of Jesus, we find a Man with whom God shares his glory. When Herod accepted the worship of the people and failed to give praise to God, he was struck down, eaten by worms and died[5]. But when Thomas said to Jesus "My Lord and my God", Jesus commended him for his belief[6]. When an angel appeared to John and he fell at his feet to worship him, the angel said "Do not do it! I am a fellow servant with you and with your brothers who hold to the testimony of Jesus. Worship God!"[7] . But when Jesus confronted John, John fell at his feet as though dead and heard those breathtaking

[1] 1Thess 1:9-10

[2] Genesis 1:26

[3] Similar references to God using plural language can be found in Gen 3:22; 11:7 and Isa 6:8

[4] Gen 1:2; Neh 9:20; Ps 139:7; Isa 63: 10-14; Prov 8:22ff; Ps 33:6; Gen 18; Ex 3:2-6; Judges 13.

[5] Acts 13:20-24

[6] John 20:28,29

[7] Rev 19:10

24

words of Jesus: "I am the First and the Last, the Living One"[1].

Research

Look up the following texts to see what light they cast on Jesus' divinity:

Mark 2:1-12

Acts 7:59

Revelation 5:12

Colossians 2:9

Colossians 1:15-19

Within the New Testament, we find the three persons of the Godhead linked together in a unity that is blasphemous if each is not God. Baptism takes place in the name of Father, Son and Holy Spirit. But each of these persons are called God[2].

Sometimes the word 'God' is used to refer to the Father alone, while at other times it refers to all three persons in the divine being. Similarly the word 'LORD' (that is, 'Yahweh') can sometimes refer to the Father, sometimes to the three persons in one

[1] Revelation 1:17-18; note how God uses almost the same phrase of himself in verse 8 of the same chapter; also compare Rev 21:6; 22:13.

[2] In Rom 9:5; Col 2:9; Titus 2:13; Heb 1:8-10;, Jesus is called God. In 2Cor 3:17; John 15:26; 1 Cor 6:19; Rom 8:9-11, the Spirit is identified as God. Of course the Father is also God, indeed the God of our Lord Jesus (Eph 1:3,17.

[1] Rom 10:13 quotes
Joel 2, Philippians 2:9-
11 quotes Isaiah 45,
John 12 quotes Isa 6,
Heb 1:10-12 quotes Ps
102, and Eph 4:8
quotes Ps 68

God, and sometimes to Jesus. Within the Old Testament, the LORD is God and God is the LORD. There is only one God and one LORD. However, many of the Old Testament references to the LORD/Yahweh are applied in the New Testament to Jesus[1].

The Biblical understanding is that God is one and unique, and at the same time three persons—the Father, Son and Holy Spirit—living and inter-relating in undivided unity. Their complex unity is seen not only in their persons, and the titles they are given, but in the work they do. All three persons of the Godhead are involved in creation and redemption. The Father sends the Son and the Son seeks to do the will of the Father, and both the Father and the Son give the Spirit to us. The Father wasn't crucified—the Son was. There is a distinction between the persons of the triune God, but never a division, for the Father is in the Son, as the Son is in the Spirit.

Christian Embarrasment

Christians have too often been defensive and negative about the doctrine of the Trinity. We feel the need to apologise for believing something for which we can find no parallels or analogies in life. Sometimes we misrepresent the Trinity by trying to manufacture analogies like the three sides of a triangle or the three leaves of a clover. These attempts invariably fail because they do not represent three persons who are each equally divine—they end up portraying three subsets, three parts of a whole. The Son is not part of God, the Son **is** God. A line, however, is only part of a triangle; it is not itself a triangle.

We should not be embarrassed. It shouldn't surprise me that God turns out to be greater and more complex than anything else I know of in this world. There are many things in this world that I find difficult to comprehend, so I should not be surprised that I cannot completely fathom the Creator of the universe. This is not to say that the Trinity is an impenetrable mystery that I cannot understand in any fashion at all. We must not confuse knowing everything with knowing something. I **can** know that God is three persons and one God. This is not hard to understand, nor difficult to accept.

Implications

It is important for Christians to spend time thinking about the Trinity and to preach it to non-Christians. In the Trinity we have the gospel of God and without the Trinity, the gospel is defective. The Trinity helps us understand ourselves and our world, as well as God and the gospel. Furthermore, the alternatives to Trinitarianism, create imponderable philosophical and ethical problems.

That God is three persons in one God means that ultimate reality is *personal* and *relational*. God is not an impersonal force, nor did he create us out of the need to love somebody. My perception of life—that personal relationships are of highest importance—is correct, for ultimate reality is not simply 'being', but three persons in eternal relationship.

The full divinity of Jesus was essential in him paying the penalty for our sins. If Jesus was not fully God, then God was punishing an innocent third party instead of the guilty. This would have been not only unjust, but ineffective—the death of a mere man, even a perfect man, could pay for no more than the sin of one other person. But if *God was in Christ* reconciling the world to himself, then God was bearing the penalty for our crime, and not for ours only but for the sins of the whole world[1]. [1] 2 Cor 5:19; Jn 2:1-2

Because Jesus is both God and man, he is able to fully represent us before his Father. He brings his brothers to glory, those with whom he shared flesh and blood[2]. [2] Hebrews 2:5-18

The interpersonal relationship of the Father, Son and Spirit demonstrates to us the nature of relational ethics. Each is equally God and yet the Son seeks to do the will of his Father, and together with the Father, sends the Spirit. 'Other-person-centredness' and loving submission are illustrated in the divine relationship. In the world created by such a God, there is an order of relationships which in no way implies inequality, but a diverse unity and harmony between equal persons.

Not to believe in the Trinity leads ultimately to a denial of the gospel. If Jesus is not God, he could not pay for our sins. If Jesus is not God, it is inappropriate for us to call him Lord, to give him our lives, to follow him, or to sing his praises. If the Spirit is not the Spirit of Christ and of God, then we do not have Christ with us as he promised. Each must equally be God and all three must be an undivided unity.

Think it Through

1 Does the doctrine of the Trinity play any part in your Christian life? Should it?

2 How might this doctrine affect the way we pray?

3 Do the different persons of the Trinity have different 'functions'? How do they interrelate?

4 How would you explain the Trinity to a Jehovah's Witness, a Jew or a Muslim?

3
Visions on the road

Two famous men came to radically different conclusions through visions they experienced on the road. At around 40 AD, Saul of Tarsus, that self-righteous Pharisee, discovered his utter worthlessness and sinfulness when confronted by Jesus on the road to Damascus. In 1749, on the road from Paris to Vincennes, Jean Rousseau also experienced a vision. In that trance he saw that man is naturally good and that it is our institutions that make us wicked.

These two visions could not be more different, and they stand as symbols of the conflict of thought within our society. One is a vision of revelation, where interaction with the personal Creator leads to a realisation of personal sinfulness. The other is a trance where man, upon reflection, excuses himself of guilt and establishes his innocence. Evangelical faith is committed to the truth of:

The universal sinfulness and guilt of human nature since the Fall, rendering man subject to God's wrath and condemnation.

This is the fourth statement of the AFES doctrinal basis.

Since Rousseau's day the atheists of our society have tried to argue for the goodness of man. They have tinkered with our social structures, hoping to reduce their negative influence on man's otherwise good nature. They have tried one educational system after another and have undertaken their revolutions in the name of liberty, fraternity and equality. Yet the optimistic humanism which assumes that man is fundamentally good is constantly denied by the facts of human experience. The tide of war, crime, inhumanity, self-centredness and greed has never been turned stemmed by better education, better housing, more democratic structures, access to the courts, free and universal education, or any of these reforms. These schemes and institutions are not wrong in themselves, but the romantic hope that they would reveal man's innate goodness and bring on the utopia, has been shown to be the fraud that it always was.

However, even today the obvious alternative view, that man is himself fundamentally marred and immoral, is not allowed a hearing in the humanities. There are several reasons for this

29

censorship. Firstly, we can change structures and institutions, but we do not know how to change the human heart. Secondly, to claim that all men everywhere are immoral is to claim that I am immoral, and that is too painful and insulting. As the psalmist says of the godless: "In his own eyes he flatters himself too much to detect or hate his sin"[1]. Thirdly, to claim that man is immoral will require some establishment of morality, some absolute which will rule over man and dethrone him from his claim to supremacy.

The easiest way to get rid of temptation is to give in. The easiest way to get rid of the notion of sin is to abolish God. The atheist closes his eyes and hopes that sin will disappear, but he must keep his eyes closed or the facts of human sinfulness will overwhelm him.

[1] Ps 36:2

Universality

Breathing, eating and drinking aside, there are few, if any, conscious actions of any significance which all humans share. However, the Bible argues that all people everywhere, and each and every person within humanity, sins[2]. The psalmist asks the rhetorical question: "If you, O LORD, kept a record of sins, O Lord, who could stand?"[3]. As the proverb also says: "Who can say, 'I have kept my heart pure; I am clear and without sin?'"[4]. The universal nature of our sinfulness is assumed.

Paul argues that this universality of sin flows from the actions of Adam in the Garden[5]. There is a solidarity in our humanity that the Scripture does not seek to explain, but simply upholds—the whole human race is sinful.

This solidarity does not mean that individuals are not responsible for their sinfulness. Even Adam's son, Cain, was challenged to resist temptation, and was held responsible for his own choices when he gave way to temptation and murdered his brother[6]. Both the individualism by which I am responsible for my own choices and the solidarity by which I am affected by the context of my existence, are affirmed in the Scriptures. Conversely, the extremes of individualism, which argue for my autonomy, and the extremes of solidarity, which absolve me from responsibility, are denied by the Scriptures.

[2] 1 Kings 8:46; Rom 3:9-20; Luke 11:13; Eph 2:1-3; 1 Jn 1:8-10.
[3] Ps 130:3
[4] Prov 20:9

[5] Rom 5:12-21; 1 Cor 15:21-22

[6] Gen 4:6-11

Definition Sin is a commonly misunderstood concept in our society, for it requires a clear understanding of God. It is a personal and relational word, not a legal one.

There are many words in the Bible that can be translated 'sin', but we will not understand the Biblical concept simply by analysing the definition of these words. The concept of sin is spelt out in the events of Genesis 2 & 3, and it always entails opposition to God. Sin is not to be seen only in action, but rather in the derivation of that action—the motivation and nature that gives rise to the action.

In the Garden, Adam and Eve ate of the fruit of the tree of the knowledge of good and evil. This was a temptation to become like God, knowing good and evil. It was a temptation that was half true. In Genesis 3:22 we read that they *did* become "like one of us knowing good and evil". However, because man is not God, such a state was intolerable. God could not allow it and so excluded man from the fellowship of the Garden and from access to the tree of life. The nature of sin is that we who are created in the image and likeness of God should seek to become God.

1. An attempted coup

In Romans 1:18-32 sin is explained in terms of not giving thanks to God or acknowledging him. In accepting this lie as the basis of life, man's nature is fundamentally changed. Now he no longer lives in relationship with God as his God, but lives in rebellion. And this rebellion leads him to the immorality and decadence that we see all around us.

2. Rebels

Thus the Scriptures see that our very natures are sinful. Our actions are the actions of our sinful nature[1]. Jesus says that sin does not come from 'outside' but from within, from our own hearts. "For from within, out of men's hearts, come evil thoughts, sexual immorality, theft, murder, adultery, greed, malice, deceit, lewdness, envy, slander, arrogance and folly. All these evils come from inside and make a man unclean"[2]. This sinfulness of our human nature is consistently taught throughout the Scriptures[3]. James also teaches us that temptation comes from within: "But each one is tempted when by his own evil desire, he is dragged away and enticed. Then after desire has conceived, it gives birth to sin; and sin when it is full grown gives birth to death"[4].

[1] Eph 2:3; Rom 1:24,28

[2] Mark 7:15-23

[3] Gen 6:5; 8:21; Isa 29:13; Jer 17:9

[4] James 1:14-15

Research

Study the following passages and list what they tell us about man's natural standing with God.

Romans 8:5-8

Colossians 1:21

Isaiah 64:6

1 Corinthians 2:14

2 Corinthians 4:4

Ephesians 2:2

John 8:34

This enmity with God is a two-way warfare—God is angry with our sinfulness. The devil, of course, wants us to think otherwise. Ever since that barefaced lie he told Eve—"You will not surely die"—he has been seeking to persuade men that God will not be angry with the sinner or bring judgement on those who continue in sinfulness. Three times Paul warns us of this attempt to delude us into thinking that sinfulness has no negative consequences. "Do not be deceived", he writes, "Neither the sexually immoral, nor idolaters, nor male prostitutes, nor homosexual offenders, nor thieves, nor the greedy, nor drunkards, nor slanderers, nor swindlers will inherit the kingdom of God"[1]. "Let no one deceive you with empty words, for because of such things God's wrath comes on those who are disobedient"[2]. "I warn you as I did before that those who live like this will not inherit the kingdom of God".[3]

Sin will pay its wages, and its wages are death[4]. The wrath

[1] 1 Cor 6:9-10

[2] Eph 5:6
[3] Gal 5:21
[4] Rom 6:23; Gen 2:17

or anger of God is revealed from heaven against all godlessness.[1] There will be in the future a day of wrath, of God's wrath, when "his righteous judgement will be revealed"[2]. The whole of humanity is living under the sentence of death.[3]

[1] Gal 5:21
[2] Rom 2:5
[3] Rom 5:12-15; 1Cor 15:21-22

Getting the doctrine right

Many problems in Christian living and evangelism stem from misunderstanding the doctrine of sin. There have been long theological debates and controversies on the subject. It is a distinctly Christian and Biblical doctrine, and Bible believers should not be in great confusion over this teaching.

It is important to see sin as breaking the covenant relationship with God, rather than simply breaking the law. Through the law we become conscious of sin and the law may even educate me about sin[4]. However, sin is not just breaking laws, but rebelling against the Lawmaker.[5]

[4] Rom 3:20; 7:7-12
[5] cf 1 Jn 3:4

Sin is also not to be seen purely as overt actions. It is our heart and mind that are rebellious against God and give rise to actions. The actions are to sin what symptoms are to a disease.

It is also important to understand sin as being in opposition towards *God*[6]. The actions of sinfulness may be anti-social, but the essence of sinfulness is the rejection of God. Arguing on the subject of Christian liberty, Paul goes so far as to say "Everything that does not come from faith is sin".[7]

[6] Ps 51:4; Rom 8:7

[7] Rom 14:23

While our nature is sinful, we must not conclude that we are without guilt. We are responsible for choosing to follow our nature. I still have a will which is challenged to choose God and repent and a conscience that can excuse or accuse me.[8] I never sin 'against my will'—my will consents to every sin I commit. Being neither a puppet nor a programmed machine, my sinful choices reflect my own heart's desires. Both my choices and my desires bring God's righteous condemnation upon me.

[8] Josh 24:15; Mk 1:15; Rom 2: 14-15

We must be wary of minimising man's corruption. Many people have sought to reduce the impact of the Bible's teaching by retaining something of the goodness of man. This goodness, it is hoped, will be fanned into a morality that will somehow save him. Again sin is reduced to law-breaking, rather than relationship-breaking. The law-breaking is minimised with the hope that law-keeping will somehow pay for the transgressions. Such views fly in the face of passages like James 2:10 "For whoever keeps the whole law and yet stumbles at just one point is guilty of breaking all of it" or Luke 17:10 "So you also, when you have done everything you were told to do, should say, 'We are unworthy servants; we have only done our duty.'"

God's anger against sin must never be minimised. Frequently people wish to depersonalise sin so that they can depersonalise the judgement upon sin. This system of thought reduces sin to breaking the law and judgement to paying the law's requirements. But sin is rebellion against God and God is angry with sin. The Bible talks about "the wrath of God coming because of sin"[1]. It is important to see God as personally involved and concerned for his world. It is out of his love for his creation that God's anger is roused. His anger brings into stunning clarity his love in the death of Jesus on our behalf.

[1] Col 3:6

The importance of this doctrine

A right doctrine of sin will only come through a right understanding of God. However, a right doctrine of sin is necessary if we are to understand the gospel properly. Only with a right doctrine of sin will man see his need of deliverance from slavery. A wrong doctrine of sin will show man in need of inspiration to live a better life, of not needing salvation at all. A wrong doctrine of sin will make the death of Jesus obsolete.

However, for Christian living, a right doctrine of sin is essential. We must understand how totally sinful our own nature is. We must realise that it is by the power of God alone that we can be regenerated and transformed to live in holiness and righteousness. Our continued trust in the salvation of God will be undermined if we see ourselves as moral and upright.

Think it through

1   What is the normal understanding of the word 'sin'?

2   What is the Biblical definition of sin?

3   How might a mis-perception of sin affect the Christian pursuit of holiness?

4   What areas of sin do you need to address in your own life?

5   In evangelism, what aspects of sin are important to communicate to the non-Christian?

4

An unnecessary truth?

In this series of study papers we have been looking at the basic doctrines of Christianity—the important things, the things that define Evangelicalism. It is not always easy to isolate which doctrines are fundamental and essential and which are peripheral.

'Jesus is Lord', for example, is obviously essential to any understanding of what Christianity is. That he lived in Galilee is not. Of course, the Scriptures say that Jesus lived in Galilee, and to deny this would seem strange for anyone professing to live under the authority of God's Word. However, it is not one of the cardinal points of Christian doctrine.

The fourth of our doctrinal statements is a little like this. All Christians will rightly concur with this statement, although it has no great place in the basic structure of Christian thinking.

The conception of Jesus Christ by the Holy Spirit and his birth of the virgin Mary.

This statement accurately summarises the Bible's teaching about Jesus' conception and birth. And Christians have been committed to this truth for nearly two thousand years. All the same, it is a strangely unnecessary belief—unnecessary in the sense that no other doctrine hangs upon it.

It is slightly unusual, then, to have this particular statement in our list of fundamental Christian truths. When it was formed in 1936, the AFES (known then as the Inter-Varsity Fellowship) adopted the doctrinal basis of the English IVF, with the addition of this article on the virgin birth. We may never know the reasons for its inclusion in the AFES basis, although we can guess. The consistent rejection of the virgin birth by theological liberals is the most likely explanation. Including an article that affirmed belief in the virgin birth would have excluded liberals from gaining office in the movement, although one would have thought that a quite a number of the other articles would have achieved this.

The Truth

To call this doctrine 'unnecessary' is in no way to doubt its truth. Scripture is unambiguous on the matter: Jesus was conceived by the Holy Spirit and born of the virgin Mary.

Some passages imply a 'strangeness' about Jesus' birth. He is called 'Mary's son' rather than 'Joseph's son'.[1] And there is the barb thrown at Jesus by the Jews when they declare that **they** are not illegitimate children![2]

[1] Mark 6:3

[2] John 8:41

However, the basis for our knowledge of the virgin birth is found in the first chapters of Matthew and Luke. Matthew's account is told from Joseph's perspective. We are told that "before they came together she was found to be with child through the Holy Spirit". Joseph is instructed by an angel that "what is conceived in her is from the Holy Spirit". Matthew makes the editorial comment: "All this took place to fulfil what the Lord had said through the prophet: 'The virgin will be with child and will give birth to a son, and they will call him Immanuel'—which means, 'God with us.'" Joseph responds by taking Mary home as his wife, but has no sexual union with until her after Jesus is born.[3]

[3] Matthew 1:18-25

Luke recounts Jesus' birth from Mary's perspective. "You will be with child and give birth to a son," the angel tells Mary, "and you are to give him the name Jesus. He will be great and will be called the Son of the Most High. The Lord God will give him the throne of his father David, and he will reign over the house of Jacob forever; his kingdom will never end." Upon Mary's enquiry as to how this could happen while she was still a virgin, she is told, "The Holy Spirit will come upon you and the power of the Most High will overshadow you. So the holy one to be born will be called the Son of God."[4]

[4] Luke 1:26-38

The teaching of Scripture is unmistakable—Mary remained a virgin until after Jesus' birth, and his conception was the work of the Holy Spirit.

The truth under attack

The virgin birth is frequently attacked by modern sceptics. Should any girl claim that her pregnancy was the result of divine intervention (rather than a lapse in sexual standards) her claim would no doubt be treated with some suspicion. Without believing in the Lordship of Jesus, it is hard for people to accept that a virgin could give birth to a son. It is hardly surprising that in our age of godless, mechanistic thinking people doubt the virgin birth.

Christians who are affected by this thinking try to explain away embarrassing incidents like the virgin birth (or, for that matter, the resurrection). Thus, the liberal wing of Christendom, which doubts the authority of Scripture and the possibility of miracles, needs to find some explanation for the 'mythical' story of the virgin birth. They can't come straight out and say "It's false!"—that would peel back too much of the sheep's clothing from their backs. They simply offer an alternative 'interpretation'.

Some scholars argue that Matthew wrote up the virgin birth in order to make Jesus fulfil Isaiah 7 and so fit the prophetic expectation more neatly. Others contend that Matthew misunderstood Isaiah 7 and that there was never a prediction concerning a virgin. Either way, Matthew loses. Others argue from parallels in other religions that it is merely a myth used to flesh out, as it were, the incarnation. Some claim that because the virgin birth is not mentioned elsewhere in New Testament it is a mythological accretion to the gospel. Others reply that the very fact that it doesn't play any important part in the gospel is an indication of its historical integrity.

These arguments prove very little. Ultimately, it is a case of whether you believe the gospel writers or not. Matthew and Luke are straightforward in their retelling of the events: Mary conceived Jesus as a virgin by the Holy Spirit, and remained a virgin until after Jesus' birth. This is either right or wrong—fact or invention.

This doctrine has been attacked in other generations in different ways. The Docetists, who didn't believe that Jesus was fully human, objected to it, as did the Ebionites who didn't believe in his deity. The Adoptionists, who believed that the divine logos entered Jesus at some point in his life (at his baptism perhaps) also disliked the idea of the Holy Spirit being involved in Jesus' conception. Adoptionism is still around today.

Given this history of antagonism, it is understandable that the AFES included this article in its doctrinal basis. While it is hardly a central plank in Christian thought, it is a handy litmus test (to mix metaphors) for belief in the supernatural working of God through his Spirit.

However, it is possible to affirm the virgin birth and not be Christian—the Muslims do just this. And very little hangs on this doctrine.

Biblical silence

Given its history of controversy, it is surprising to note how little the Bible makes of this subject. That it happened is clearly stated. It is also made clear that it was part of God's initiative to fulfil the prophetic expectation and establish the Davidic kingdom and save the world. However, after Matthew and Luke, nothing more is said on the matter. No other conclusions are drawn.

Christians have often confused the virgin birth with the incarnation. The Bible teaches that God became man, that Jesus was both God **and** man. Jesus is not **part** God, **part** man. He is not a semi-divine being, as if God fathered him by Mary in some kind of sexual union. In pagan myth, the gods often came down to earth to sire children by human mothers, the resultant offspring being semi-divine in nature. The New Testament distances itself from this kind of parallel.

The virgin conception and birth of Jesus is **consistent** with the incarnation, but it does not prove it. Nor is it the only way God could have acted. The Bible doesn't use the virgin birth to argue for either the divinity or humanity of Jesus.

Likewise, the New Testament does not use the virgin birth to demonstrate Jesus' sinlessness. Jesus is paralleled to Adam as a new creation of humanity, but not in relation to the virgin birth. Our solidarity with Adam, and the effect of his rebellion on our sinful nature, is not mentioned often in the Scriptures—though it is there. [1] The virgin birth is not used to explain how Jesus was unaffected by the sin of Adam.

[1] eg in Romans 5:12-21

The virgin birth is the way God acted. It fulfilled the prophecy of Isaiah concerning the way in which God would establish the new Davidic kingdom. But it has no greater theological significance than that.

Too Much of a Good Thing

Through the debate over the person of Christ (whether he was fully God and/or fully man) and the devotion of some so-called 'Christians' to Mary, the virgin birth has gained an unnatural prominence in Christian thought. Consequently, the pagans have often attacked Christianity at the point of the virgin birth, thinking they were shaking the very foundations of our religion. They never realised that they were dealing with a subject on the periphery of the Christian system.

During the 3rd-5th centuries of the Christian era, the nature of Christ's person aroused long and heated discourse. How could God be man? And how could man be God? The Council of Chalcedon in 451 A.D. concluded that Jesus was both fully God and fully man, and this has been the Christian understanding ever since . This discussion placed the narratives of the virgin birth in the context of a philosophical discussion (concerning the nature of God and humanity), an arena of which

Matthew and Luke were blissfully unaware. They no doubt believed that Jesus was fully human and fully divine, but they do not mention the issue in their accounts of Jesus' birth. It does not interest them. They are more concerned with showing how God was working out his salvation plan to establish the kingdom promised to David. The later philosophical discussions have led us to put too much weight on the virgin birth as part of the Christian intellectual framework.

However, the increased prominence of Mary has been even more significant in exaggerating the place of the virgin birth. At the Council of Chalcedon, the Greek term theotokos ("mother of God") was coined to express that Jesus was indeed fully God. If, at his birth, he was divine, then Mary could be rightly designated the "mother of God". This is a theologically accurate litmus test for a right view of Jesus' personhood. However, over time, the phrase was taken as a point of devotion to Mary. Instead of expressing the divinity of Jesus, it was used to emphasise the place of Mary—"mother of God" became "Mother of god". False views of Mary began to multiply:

- People began to pray to her, thinking that, as his mother, she would have unique access to Jesus as God.
- As devotion to her increased, and wanting to separate Jesus entirely from the sin of Adam, the idea that Mary herself was sinless became widely accepted. The doctrine of the Immaculate Conception was born.
- It was only a short step from this to the doctrine of the Assumption—that Mary rose bodily to heaven. This was not officially promulgated by the Roman Catholic Church until the mid-1950s.
- Built on a misunderstanding of her sinlessness, and possibly also on a wrong view of sex, the idea that Mary was perpetually a virgin gained currency, and was eventually promulgated by the Roman Catholic Church.
- Through a misunderstanding of the angelic greeting in Luke 1, Mary was seen to be so full of grace that she could dispense grace to other people.
- Her supposed co-operation with the Holy Spirit in the conception of Jesus ("May it be to me as you have said") led her to be viewed as having a key role in the plan of redemption. She was titled 'Co-Redemptrix'.
- For many people, Mary became their Mediator—the object of prayers and devotion, and the dispenser of the grace of the gospel.
- Called the 'Queen of Heaven' she is still seen by many

today as the centre of Christian devotion.

This catalogue of 'Maryolatry' is an appalling blasphemy. It is a travesty of the gospel and it deeply offends all true Bible-believers. The virgin birth has been a critical part of this web of false thinking. The central figure in the virgin birth narrative becomes the virgin, rather than the divine child she bears.

Christians shake their heads in disbelief at the doctrines of Mary that have arisen over the centuries. What is even more remarkable is that these false views are anticipated and dealt with in the gospels themselves.

Research

Matthew 1:18-25
Mark 6:2-3
Luke 1:26-56
Luke 11:27-28
Luke 8:19-21

Look up these references and see how they relate to:

Mary's 'perpetual virginity'

Devotion to Mary

Her 'sinlessness'

Her place in Jesus' ministry

What to make of the doctrine

We must believe what God has revealed to us. The Bible records the details of the life of Jesus, even though they might not be relevant to his saving work. It is important that those who trust in Christ trust also in the Word of God about him, which includes his conception by the Holy Spirit and virgin birth.

The deity and humanity of Jesus do not require the virgin birth, but are quite consistent with this means of him coming into the world. In light of Genesis 3:15 it is not surprising that God chose to send his Son into the world to be born of a woman, to be fully human. Isaiah's prophecy that a virgin would give birth to a child who would be called 'God with us' fits nicely with the doctrine of the full divinity of Jesus.

The most important emphasis is that God was taking the initiative to save mankind by sending his eternal Son into our world. Jesus was not an enlightened human, who climbed Olympus on our behalf to bring us the knowledge of God. He is God, come from his father, to make him known to us.[1] The virgin birth is the divine signal of the dawn of the new age.

[1] cf. John 1:1-18

Think it through

Why should we defend the truth of the virgin birth?

What does the Bible make of the virgin birth?

Why is prayer to Mary unnecessary and blasphemous?

Can we be more blessed than Mary?

Other notes

5

The importance of being obstreperous

Obstreperous is a lovely word—that is, once you have learnt how to spell it! It has such an onomatopoeic hostility to it. The word means "resisting control in a noisy manner", and it is truly an evangelical term. Evangelicals must be obstreperous.

Evangelicalism is an exclusive theological position. It claims to be right and (by definition) declares all others wrong. Other more permissive views accept each other readily enough, but they cannot tolerate Evangelicalism. For Evangelicalism to survive, it must continually "resist control" by making great noise about its distinctives.

Perhaps the chief distinctive of Evangelicalism is the doctrine of redemption. The doctrine of the cross of Jesus lies at the heart of Evangelicalism, and is a sticking point for attempts at ecumenism, or Christian relativism, or syncretism. It is our insistent noisiness about the cross that makes us so obstreperous.

Many claim to "believe in the cross", but Evangelicals want to go one step further by asserting that the cross is central and fundamental to every other doctrine of Scripture. It was at this point that the English Inter-Varsity Fellowship (IVF) came into existence in 1910 in opposition to the Student Christian Movement. The difference between the two groups was not over belief in the cross, but over the centrality of the cross. Robert Horn's account of the incident makes interesting reading.[1]

[1] R.M. Horn " Student Witness and Christian Truth" (IVP)

The IVF in Australia is now known as the Australian Fellowship of Evangelical Students (AFES). The fifth of the statements of the AFES doctrinal basis is:

Redemption from the guilt, penalty, and power of sin, only through the sacrificial death, as our Representative and Substitute, of Jesus Christ, the incarnate Son of God.

This doctrinal statement does not occur in isolation, but in the

45

context of the eleven statements forming the AFES doctrinal basis. From the doctrine of Scripture (in the first statement), the doctrine of sin (in the third statement) and the understanding of God (spelt out in the second statement), the doctrine of redemption is derived. That is, without the doctrine of Scripture we would never think of either sin or redemption. Without the doctrine of God, we would have no-one to sin against, as well as no one to redeem us. Without the doctrine of sin, the doctrine of redemption would seem quite strange. However, given the previous doctrinal statements, the fifth makes excellent sense and gives rise to a totally new way of viewing the world.

Definitions

This doctrinal statement has several technical terms. Before grasping the essence of the statement itself, or seeing its implications, we need to be sure of the meaning of these terms.

1. Redemption

Redemption is a word of escape. It is about freeing or delivering people caught in some bondage. In the ancient world, the word was used in the slave markets to describe purchasing the freedom of slaves, although it has been a matter of debate as to whether it always carries with it the sense of payment of a price. The classic Old Testament redemption is that of the Israelite slaves of Egypt who were delivered under the ministry of Moses.

Within the gospel, it is clear that there is always the payment of the price, namely the death of Jesus. The idea of redemption is expressed in phrases like "gave his life as a ransom for many"[1]; "justified freely by his grace through the redemption that came by Christ Jesus"[2]; and "in him we have redemption through his blood, the forgiveness of sins"[3].

[1] Mark 10:45

[2] Romans 3:24
[3] Ephesians 1:7

The captivity from which we need redemption is that of sin. It was Jesus himself who said "I tell you the truth, everyone who sins is a slave to sin"[4]. Sin holds us captive through our guilt, through the penalty that sin brings upon us, and through the power of sin over us.

[4] John 8:34

2. Guilt, Penalty and power

Our guilt often issues in feelings of guilt, but stands true even when we are unconscious of our guiltiness. It is the work of the Spirit to convict the world of its guilt[5], and it is the temptation of those who walk in darkness to say that they have not sinned[6]. But whether we feel guilty, or have been convicted of guilt by the Spirit, we are objectively guilty. Furthermore, we are suffering and shall suffer the penalty for our sin—the wrath of God. This

[5] John 16:8
[6] 1 John 1:8,10

wrath is already revealed from heaven against sinfulness[1] and is being stored up for the great day of wrath.[2] In the meantime we live under the power or dominion of sin. The power/dominion is the law which declares us to be the objects of God's wrath.[3] The dominion of sin also has to do with "the ruler of the kingdom of the air" who is at work in the disobedient.[4] And the dominion of sin involves the cravings of our sinful nature whereby we live out our sinfulness.[5]

[1] Romans 1:18-32

[2] Romans 2:5

[3] 1 Cor 15:56

[4] Ephesians 2:2

[5] Ephesians 2:3

3. Sacrificial death

The sacrificial death of Jesus is the subject of this doctrinal statement about redemption. It is not just that Jesus died, but that he died as a sacrifice for sins. Redemption was not achieved by the life of Jesus, but through the death of Jesus. Jesus' death, then, was not simply an example of love or martyrdom, but a sacrifice for sins. The Old Testament gave clear meaning to this term 'sacrifice', which the New Testament takes and applies to the death of Jesus.

Research

Study the following passages to see how the Old Testament imagery of sacrifice is applied to Jesus.

Exodus 12:1-42; 1 Corinthians 5:7

Leviticus 16; Hebrews 9:1-10:18; Romans 3:25

4. Representative and substitute

To make the character of Jesus' sacrificial death perfectly clear and unambiguous, our doctrinal statement has continued with a phrase in parenthesis describing Jesus as our Representative and Substitute. This has to be spelt out, for some people accept the sacrificial death of Jesus, but then reinterpret it in their own quite different terms.

Some see it as a sacrifice of love, setting an example for us to follow, and this is true to an extent.[1] Others stress that Jesus made satisfaction for our failure to keep the law. Still others emphasise that through his death he conquered the powers and principalities of evil. These are all true in themselves, but inadequate. Only by seeing Jesus as our substitute do we see the full impact of his death on the cross.

[1] 1 Peter 2:21-25; Romans 5:8

He is our representative in that when one died for all, all died.[2] He is the advocate who speaks to the Father on our behalf by his sacrificial death.[3] It was as our substitute that he represented us. He gave his life as a ransom for many.[4] "God made him who knew no sin to be sin for us, so that in him we might become the righteousness of God".[5] "Christ died for sins once for all, the righteous for the unrighteous, to bring you to God."[6] "He himself bore our sins in his body on the tree ... by his wounds you have been healed."[7] In passage after passage of Scripture, the only satisfactory explanation is that Jesus died as our substitute.

[2] 2 Cor 5:14
[3] 1 John 2:1
[4] Mark 10:45

[5] 2 Cor 5:21
[6] 1 Peter 3:18

[7] 1 Peter 2:24

5. The incarnate Son of God

The final phrase of the doctrinal statement is the description of Jesus as the incarnate Son of God. The phrase 'Son of God' does not always mean God, the Son. Frequently in the New Testament it means the Messiah. However, when it is prefixed by the word 'incarnate' it has its full theological significance of God the Son become man. This is critical in describing the sacrificial death of Jesus because if Jesus is not incarnate—is not fully human—he cannot be our representative. And if Jesus is not fully divine, he is not qualified to be our substitute. If he was simply a human, even a perfect human, then his death could only pay for the sin of one other human. Furthermore, God would be immoral for punishing an innocent third party in order to allow the guilty second party to be justified.

However, God was in Christ reconciling the world to himself.[8] In Christ the whole fullness of God was pleased to dwell in order to reconcile to himself all things.[9] Thus God takes upon himself the sinfulness of mankind. It is God who puts forward the sacrifice of atonement.[10] God turns aside God's anger by God paying the penalty for man's sin. Certainly Jesus had to be man in order to be a genuine substitute, but to pay for the sins of

[8] 2 Cor 5:18,19
[9] Col 1:18,19; 2:9,10

[10] Romans 3:25

the whole world...only God could do such a thing.

Therefore there is no blasphemy or polytheism when Paul writes "He died for all, that those who live should no longer live for themselves, but for him who died for them and was raised again."[1] If Christ is not God, it is totally inappropriate for us to live for him. If Christ is God then we can live for no other.

[1] 2 Cor 5:15

The Most Important Word — only

Standing back from these technical definitions, we need to see the overall thrust of the sentence. The key word in the sentence turns out not to be a technical word but a little word—'only'.

It is only through the sacrificial death of Jesus that we can have redemption from sin. In a sense, the word 'only' is unnecessary. If we rightly understand the redemption from sin described in this statement, we know that it could only come this way. If God the Son has himself paid the penalty for our sins, what other sacrifice could be sufficient or necessary to bring about redemption? Surely if there was an easier way, God the Father would have heard his Son's plea in the Garden of Gethsemane and offered up some lesser sacrifice![2]

[2] Mark 14:32-42

However, many people will accept that Jesus died as a sacrifice for sin, but will not acknowledge that this is the only way for redemption. Some want an alternative route to the Father, even though Jesus said that there was only one Way. [3]

[3] John 14:6

The word 'only' excludes all human merit. There is nothing we can do to free ourselves from the guilt, penalty, dominion and pollution of sin. If there was, then Jesus' sacrificial death was unnecessary.[4] If we do all that is required of us, and obey God perfectly, we are still but unworthy servants simply doing our duty.[5] We cannot accrue good works to counter our huge debit balance before God. As one Christian Teacher put it, this is akin to not paying for some item purchased and then expecting the shopkeeper to cancel the debt because we successfully pay for the next item we purchase. Even the holiness that we enjoy issues from the cross of Jesus, rather than leading to the cross of Jesus. It is only by the one, perfect sacrifice offered by our great high priest that we have been liberated from the continual offering of ineffective sacrifices.[6]

[4] Galatians 2:21

[5] Luke 17:10

[6] Hebrews 7-10

The exclusive nature of 'only'

Once we understand the central thrust of this doctrinal statement as declaring the sole means of redemption, we can begin to see why Evangelicalism is so exclusive. If the only means of redemption is the sacrificial death of the incarnate Son of God, then any alternative or additional means of redemption is an attack on our redemption, an attack on the sacrificial death of Jesus, an attack on the incarnate Son of God himself.

For example, Paul says "There is one God and one mediator between God and men, the man Jesus Christ, who gave himself as a ransom for all men."[1] When people suggest that we turn to other mediators between God and man—whether priests or saints or Mary—they are expressing dissatisfaction, wittingly or unwittingly, with the one true mediator and his sacrificial death. Additional mediators are a direct contradiction of this verse. However, additional mediators are also a direct contradiction of the theology that lies behind this verse—that the sacrificial death of the incarnate Son of God is the only way of redemption. Thus Evangelicals must attack all use of saints, of the dead, of priests, and of Mary, as a means or channel by which we can approach God. We cannot compromise on these issues without compromising the redemption that was won for us by Jesus.

[1] 1 Tim 2:5,6

Each of the main theological alternatives to Evangelicalism within Christianity denies this doctrinal statement. Frequently they deny it unwittingly and in practice, rather than intentionally and theoretically.

1. Liberals

The Liberals (theologically speaking) are a good example. Some from a liberal theological viewpoint quite specifically and intentionally query the divinity of Jesus or the substitutionary nature of his atoning death, or the reality of the guilt, penalty, dominion and pollution of sin. They are openly preaching an alternative gospel.

However, a liberal theology which puts its emphasis on the reforming of mankind by setting an example of love and by agitating for social justice can be denying our redemption just as effectively. They downplay the need for a spiritual redemption from sin and the wrath of God. This is not to say that Evangelicals will be unconcerned about social justice, but that we cannot be confused about the relative importance of social justice and spiritual redemption. To use redemption language ('liberation', 'deliverance') of the political struggles of oppressed people is to seriously confuse the gospel.

2. Ritualists

Similarly, when ritualists—be they Anglo-Catholic, Roman Catholic, Orthodox or whatever—establish church in the terms of temple worship (with priests and sacrifices and altars) there is a serious confusion about the nature of our redemption. Many

50

people involved in these traditions do not mean any disloyalty, but rather honour to the Lord Jesus who has died to save them. However, when we talk about offering up the holy sacrifice, or of every mass going to plea for pardon, or we call upon people to bow before the symbols of the sacrificial Jesus and to confess their sins to priests (who have power to declare absolution), or we think that worshipping God means conducting a certain kind of church service—then the great truth of the redemption is at best confused, and at worst lost completely.

3. Experientialists

The experientialists are much the same. Those who find the worship and service of God in their present experiences of him, whether through meditation or aesthetics or ecstasy or some super-rational or arational activity, do not approach God on the basis of redemption. Again we find many of these people do believe in the redemption of the Lord Jesus Christ. However, in reality they base their assurance of relationship with God on the overwhelming experience of his presence that they have.

The way that they have received this experience varies from tradition to tradition. It may be by saying the Jesus prayer in the Orthodox tradition, or by reciting the Rosary in the Catholic tradition, or through liturgical dance or being slain in the Spirit or... Whatever the means, they have more confidence in their experience than in the Lord Jesus, who has died to bring them into God's presence. Their faith rests not upon the death of Jesus, but upon having 'the experience'. And their acceptance of fellow believers is based upon whether the fellow believer has had 'the experience'.

But our acceptance with God, our relationship with him, is based upon the death of Jesus on our behalf. Sin is not breaking rules; it is being off-side with God. We do not become on-side with God by going through extraordinary experiences, but by God paying the penalty for us in the death of his Son. This is appropriated through faith, not through experiences, any more than through good works.

4. Other religions

Just as redemption marks us out from other so-called Christian theologies, so it also distinguishes us from other religions. The sacrificial death of the incarnate Son of God is at the very heart of Jewish and Islamic rejection of Christianity. Both groups reject that he is the incarnate Son of God and that he could be a sacrifice for sin. The Muslims even reject the idea that he died at all. They have no problems about him rising to be with the Father. The Jews reject the idea of his resurrection, though accepting his death.

Evangelicals losing their way

There is no point more central to Evangelical faith than the redemption that has been won for us in Christ. However, Evangelicals are frequently seduced away from this great truth. How can it possibly happen?

One of the great problems with redemption is taking it for granted. We resent being told the old, old story yet again. We think we know all about the cross, and as we take our eyes and minds and attention away from it, we are easily deceived. We need to continue to think and reflect on the great love of God for us in Christ's death on our behalf.

Once we take the cross of Christ for granted, we start to assume that others who profess Christ believe as we do that Jesus has died for sin. They frequently *say* they believe it, and in their hearts they may mean and intend that they do. However, the full articulate view of the substitutionary and representative death of Jesus as the only method of redemption from the guilt, penalty and power of sin—this is not what they mean when they say they believe that Jesus died for sin. Thus we enter into fellowship with people who have a different view of the cross.

This subtle compromise leads us to accept practices that are inconsistent with the doctrine of redemption. We are usually not seduced by full, frontal argument, for the teaching of Scripture is perfectly clear. But we do get seduced into accepting practices that are inconsistent with the Bible. We join up with a church that treats its minister as a priest; or we begin to emphasise the social implications of the gospel and start to move with people who do not believe in the gospel at all; or we fellowship with people whose basis of assurance lies in experience not in the cross of Jesus. Each of these groups will say that they believe in the death of Jesus, but in their additions to it, they are denying its sufficiency. After a while we adopt their additions to the cross and become attached to them as significant and important to our spiritual life. Thus we have the inconsistency of Evangelicals meditating in yoga fashion, trying to get in touch with the great spiritual reality!

Christless Christianity and Crossless Christianity are not Christianity at all. Christ and his cross cannot be on the fringe of Christianity. Authentic Christianity has the cross of Jesus solidly and unequivocally at the centre.

Is that enough noise?

Think it through

1   What are some of the different ways people interpret Jesus' death?

2   What is meant by the Biblical term 'redemption'? Think of some metaphors or illustrations to communicate the concept in today's terms.

3   Compromise comes not from denial but from pushing the cross off centre. In what ways do we see 'Christian' groups, movements or church programmes do that today?

4   Athanasius argued for the divinity of Jesus from his work of salvation. Can you guess his line of argument?

Other Notes

6

Pitiful Christians

Over nineteen centuries ago, Paul wrote to some sceptical Christians: "If only for this life we have hope in Christ, we are to pitied more than all men."[1] Many non-Christians pity the pathetic creatures called Christians. They pity us for our weakness of mind and our superstitious beliefs, not least of all our belief in the resurrection. But for Paul, it was the exact reverse— we are to be pitied if there is no resurrection.

[1] 1 Corinthians 15:19

The resurrection of Jesus from the dead is central to the Christian message. Without this resurrection Christianity is useless, false and futile, and Christians are still in their sins, lost, and pitiful![2] When the book of Acts records gospel preaching, the one element that is always included is the resurrection of Jesus. In Athens, Paul's gospel is summarised as "preaching the good news of Jesus and the resurrection".[3] Without this resurrection, there can be no gospel.

[2] 1 Cor 15:14-19

[3] Acts 17:18

Pagan Christians

How then can a Bishop, theologian, or any Christian for that matter, deny the resurrection? If the resurrection is so central to Christianity, then surely denial of the resurrection should lead to a total renunciation of Christianity. For people to continue in Christian ministry and public Christian leadership while denying the resurrection seems contradictory. How can it be?

Firstly, we must put this in perspective. The media's exposure of heretics and radicals draws our attention to Bishops or theologians who deny the resurrection. When a Bishop speaks of his *belief* in the resurrection, it is not recorded in the newspapers. The news is a manufactured commodity which doesn't necessarily reflect reality. We must not assume that all theologians or Bishops deny the resurrection.

But the question remains: How can anyone continue in the role of Christian leadership and deny that Jesus is risen from the dead? The answer lies in theological double-talk; it all depends on what you mean by 'resurrection'. The New Testament is so explicit about the importance of the resurrection that even those who deny it declare that they believe it. They simply reinterpret the meaning of the word 'resurrection' so as to make their belief consistent with Christian profession. But how can you redefine a word like 'resurrection'? The Macquarie dictionary gives us five different definitions, all of which clearly refer to the idea of rising again from the dead. What is there to define or redefine?

Since the Second World War, it has become popular to 'demythologise' the New Testament—that is, to remove its legendary or mythological elements and so restate its teaching in rational terms for modern man. It is an attempt to translate the New Testament out of the cultural thoughts and terms of the first century into the cultural concepts of the 20th century. The aim of this is not to deny the teaching of the New Testament, but rather to re-express it in a way that is meaningful in the contemporary world.

It is argued, in this instance, that the Apostles' experience of the continuing impact of Jesus upon their life after his death, was expressed in terms of the myth of the dying and rising God. Because modern man in his scientific technology cannot accept such mythological ideas, we must describe the New Testament experience in new terms and ways that do not rely on the resurrection myth. This will give people 'resurrection faith', that is, faith like the New Testament faith, without being caught up in the details of a legendary story. To believe that the resurrection was an historical fact is to believe in the historical fact of the Good Samaritan or the Prodigal Son—it is to miss the point of the story by confusing fact and fiction. Or so it is argued.

Today there are Christian leaders who profess their belief in the resurrection, and in resurrection faith, but believe that Jesus' body lies a'mouldering in a Palestinian grave.

A painless appendectomy

Christian reaction to leaders who deny the resurrection has been relatively quiet. There have been mild protests at the appointments of some men. There have been a few letters to newspapers disassociating ourselves from such teaching. A couple of times heresy trials have been conducted, but on each occasion the heretics have won the day. Again we must ask why this is so, and by the end of this paper the answer may become clear.

Evangelicals firmly believe in the word of God and have thus always committed themselves to the view that Jesus rose from the dead. This is expressed in the sixth of the doctrinal statements of the Australian Fellowship of Evangelical Students' doctrinal basis:

The bodily resurrection of Jesus Christ from the dead .

A similar commitment to the resurrection can be found in the Apostles' and Nicene creeds, the Westminster Confession of Faith and the 39 Articles.

However, for many Christians belief in the resurrection has become an *appendix* to their theological thinking. The doctrine of God and Sin and Christ's atoning work on the cross, even of his return and of our repentance and faith, have dominated Evangelical understanding of the gospel. The resurrection is a little like the virgin birth—something that we believe in, but that is not fundamental to our gospel thinking. It is an appendix that we can omit without disturbing the logic of our gospel. After all, does not Jesus call out "It is finished" at the point of his death? The resurrection seems to be little more than tying up the loose ends of the gospel story.

Allocating the resurrection to the backwater of theological thinking is out of step with the New Testament, just as out of step as reinterpreting or denying it. The 'resurrection appendix' has been painlessly removed—a minor operation—and there has been little sympathy or reaction from the Christian public.

For many Christians the resurrection has become important only as an apologetic for the existence of God. We have been encouraged to look at the evidences for the resurrection in order to come to the conclusion that God exists and that Jesus is the Christ.

It is true that in the New Testament the resurrection points to the fact that Jesus is the Christ. However, this is not done to demonstrate that Jesus is powerful or that the supernatural exists. In the New Testament the resurrection points to the way in which Jesus fulfils Old Testament expectations.

The weakness of Christian belief in the resurrection has been a sad testimony to our lack of understanding of the gospel and has led us to easy defeat at the hands of the false teachers within Christianity.

What is the resurrection?

To believe, as our doctrinal statement puts it, in "the bodily resurrection of Jesus Christ from the dead" is to accept that he came back to life again after death. To put it in the words of the fourth of the 39 articles:

> *Christ did truly rise again from death, and took again his body, with flesh, bones, and all things appertaining to*

[1] The 39 Articles of Religion form the doctrinal statement of the Anglican Church throughout the world.

the perfection of Man's nature; wherewith he ascended into Heaven, and there sitteth, until he return to judge all men on the last day.[1]

The resurrection is different from the idea of the immortality of the soul, whereby the spirit or soul leaves the body to go into an incorporeal state of being. It is different from reincarnation, in which the soul passes from one body into another body, be it human or animal, and thus continues through the cycle of birth and maturation and death. And it is far different from the idea of annihilation, whereby at death the person simply disintegrates to no longer exist except in peoples' memories. Resurrection simply means 'a dead person coming back to life'.

The New Testament is purposely unclear about the exact nature of the resurrection body. Paul says it is foolish to ask how the dead are raised. The body of the age to come will be different from the present body, in that the present body is attuned to the world of death and corruption whereas the body to come will be

[2] 1 Corinthians 15:35-49

glorious and spiritual.[2] The spiritual body must not be seen as spirit alone. Jesus makes a point of eating fish before his

[3] Luke 24:37-43

disciples in order to demonstrate his non-ghostly existence.[3] New Testament resurrection is bodily resurrection. However, to emphasise the details of Jesus' resurrection body indicates our lack of resurrection thinking. The emphasis of the resurrection in the Scriptures is not the miraculous nature of Jesus' bodily existence after death, but the beginning of the age to come.

Research

The resurrection in the New Testament builds upon concepts already anticipated in the Old Testament. Jesus speaks of his resurrection as being a fulfilment of the prophecies concerning the Messiah who had to suffer and rise again. He even points out the significance of the third day. Look up the following Old Testament passages to see how they anticipate the idea of Resurrection.

Ezekiel 37

Daniel 12

Hosea 6

Building on this expectation, the New Testament describes the judgement day in terms of 'The Resurrection'.[1] Paul, the good Pharisee, believes in The Resurrection, without reference to Jesus.[2] He argues from The Resurrection to Jesus' resurrection and back again.[3] Christ's resurrection is the beginning of The Resurrection—the firstfruits of those who have fallen asleep.[4] With Jesus' resurrection, the kingdom of God commences on earth, the new age begins, and the judgement of the world is established.

[1] Mark 12:23; John 25:28-30
[2] Acts 23:6-10
[3] 1 Corinthians 15:12-19
[4] 1 Corinthians 15:20ff

Paul's argument in Athens also follows this theme of linking Jesus' resurrection with the coming judgement of the world: "In the past God overlooked such ignorance, but now he commands all people everywhere to repent. For he has set a day when he will judge the world with justice by the man he has appointed. He has given proof of this to all men by raising him from the dead".[5]

[5] Acts 17:30-31

God's intention is to judge the world by a man—the Son of Man.[6] It is as a man that Jesus has risen to sit at the right hand of God in all power and authority.[7] God has now established the day upon which he will judge the world, and the proof of this is given in the resurrection of the man from death. With the resurrection of Jesus, the judge and the judgement day have been clearly identified. Thus it is in the resurrection of Jesus that we see him declared to be Messiah, Son of God, Lord and Christ.[8]

[6] Daniel 7:13ff
[7] Hebrews 2:5ff

[8] Romans 1:3,4; Acts 2:32-36

The disciples did not understand all this prior to Jesus' crucifixion.[9] Martha could only think that resurrection referred to the judgement day.[10] It was a great shock for them to perceive Jesus as 'The Resurrection'. However, after the death of Jesus, the disciples uniformly bear testimony to seeing his tomb empty and meeting with him on several occasions over forty days. They were in no doubt that it was the same man, the man who was crucified. The marks on his hands and in his side were visible. Yet Jesus was in such a glorified state they worshipped him.[11]

[9] Mark 9:10
[10] John 11:24

[11] Matthew 28:17

The subsequent preaching of the apostles about the coming of the kingdom of God, the judgement day, the Messianic claims of Christ, are all meaningless without the experience of the resurrected Jesus. They may have been liars and cooked up the story, but they were not preachers of a legendary myth, trying to express the touch of the supernatural. They preached the new age, which events had forced them to perceive as already having arrived in the person of Jesus.

The Resurrected Christian

As Jesus starts the new age of the resurrection, so Christians now participate in that new age. We have also been raised. At this stage, our resurrection is a spiritual reality—the spiritual reality of regeneration or rebirth. We have been born again by the resurrection of Jesus.[1]

With the resurrection of Jesus came the outpouring of his Spirit that led to the new birth prophesied by Ezekiel and Joel.[2] The Christian can be spoken of as having "been raised with Christ"—that is, a past tense, something that has already happened to us.[3] However, we still await the resurrection of our bodies. We await the return of Christ, when we will be raised physically and transformed from this earthly existence to the heavenly reality.[4] At this time, our spiritual resurrection cannot be seen for it has no physical counterpart—our lives are "hidden with Christ in God until he returns".[5] Thus we put up with the sufferings of a sick world and a dying body, eagerly looking forward to the hope that lies before us, the resurrection of our lowly bodies into the likeness of his glorious body.

[1] 1 Peter 1:3
[2] John 3:1ff; Exek 36:24ff; Acts 2:14ff; Joel 2:28-32
[3] Eph 2:6; Col 3:1
[4] Rom 8:18-25; Col 3:4; Phil 3:20f 1 Cor 15:23-28, 50-57 1 Thess 4:13-18
[5] Col 3:3,4; 1 Jn 3:1-3

But some doubted

When the disciples met with Jesus on the mountain prior to his departure, they worshipped him. But Matthew records that some doubted.[6] Luke tells us that Jesus recognised their doubts and that even seeing his body, they "did not believe it because of joy and amazement".[7] When Paul preached in Athens, the people listened to him until he mentioned the resurrection. "When they heard about the resurrection of the dead, some of them sneered, but others said 'We want to hear you again upon this subject'".[8]

The evidences for the resurrection are plain and open for all to see. It was "not done in a corner" as Paul reminded King Agrippa. It was also done in accordance with the prophets.[9] The witnesses do not follow cleverly devised myths, but by prophecy and history, they claim to know of the risen power of Jesus, both in his transfiguration and his death and rising again.[10]

Many attempts have been made to discount the evidences of the resurrection and Christians have been able to respond to

[6] Matt 28:17
[7] Luke 24: 38-41
[8] Acts 17:32
[9] Acts 26:26-27
[10] 2 Peter 1: 16-21; 1 John 1:1-4

these arguments with increasing confidence.[1]

However, still some people doubt. They can come in the sophisticated guise of David Hume, who had more confidence in the continued, natural event of dead men staying dead than he had in eyewitnesses. Or they can stick to the simple *a priori* argument that dead men don't rise. People find it necessary to doubt the resurrection, for belief in the resurrection inevitably leads to belief in Christ. We are often asked to provide evidence from non-Christians who saw the risen Jesus. Such a request is ludicrous. It was the resurrection that led people to become Christians.

However, there is a spiritual reason why people do not believe in the resurrection, a spiritual reason that means that all the evidences in the world will never persuade them. On the road to Emmaus, the two who travelled with Jesus did not recognise him until he opened their minds to the Scriptures.[2] To the unbelieving disciples, Jesus explained how he had fulfilled the Scriptures in his death and resurrection.[3] Earlier in Luke's gospel, we have been told that "If they do not listen to Moses and the Prophets, they will not be convinced even if someone rises from the dead".[4]

It is not until Christ pours out his Spirit into the world that people are convinced of sin and righteousness and judgement. They are convinced through his resurrection, not by his resurrection. Through his resurrection, Jesus sits at the right hand of God and pours his Spirit upon all flesh. Hearing the word of the resurrection, people may come to faith through the work of the Spirit.

[1] Frank Morrison "Who moved the stone?" (Faber); J N D Anderson "Evidences for the Ressurection" (IVP) Michael Green "Man Alive" (IVP) Josh McDowell "Evidence that demands a verdict" (Here's Life) John Stott "Basic Christianity" ch 4 (IVP)

[2] Luke 24:25-27

[3] Luke 24: 44-46

[4] Luke 16:31

Apologetics and Evangelism

Christians have been led to re-evaluate the resurrection by the lack of belief of our contemporaries. Some see the resurrection as a stumbling block that must be removed if we are to speak the contemporary language. Such removal destroys the very heart of the message, for it is by the resurrection of Jesus that we are justified.[5]

[5] Romans 4:25

For others the resurrection has become the focal point of an evidentialist apologetic, demonstrating the existence of the supernatural by the one great miraculous sign. This at least believes in the truth of the resurrection, but is also doomed to failure as it does not take into account the blindness of unbelief. Furthermore, it distorts the significance of the resurrection in New Testament theology.

This is not to say that there is no place for recounting the evidences for the resurrection. The Christian needs to see the intellectual basis for his faith. The non-Christian needs to understand what the resurrection is and the basis upon which we can know it to be true. Rehearsing the great events of the resurrection is a way of expounding the beginning of the Kingdom of God, the breaking in of the age to come, and the fulfilment of prophecy.

We must not leave the resurrection out of our evangelism. On the contrary, as we preach the resurrection we preach a central truth of the gospel of the Kingdom of God. And as people hear the word of the Cross and Resurrection of Jesus, and the Spirit of God is poured into their hearts, they will be given new life—resurrection life.

Think it through

1 Why is the resurrection central to the gospel?

2 Why can't we understand the resurrection without the Old Testament?

3 How should we use the concept of the resurrection in evangelism and apologetics?

4 What do you think Paul means in Romans 4:25 when he says that Jesus was "raised to life for our justification"?

7
Bridging the chasm of history

In the 1930s, a bridge was built across the harbour in Sydney. That bridge is still open and we can still cross it. In the first century, Jesus parted the curtain that gave us access to the Father. That curtain is still open and we can still enter in. The question is: how? How do we experience today the events of nearly 2000 years ago? It's all very well contending for the faith "that was once for all entrusted for the saints"[1], but does this make us committed to living as first century people in a twentieth century world? When I follow Christ, must I wear sandals and speak Aramaic, and go visiting houses two by two?

[1] Jude 3

Today Christians are often divided between **objectivist** and **subjectivist** theologies. To the objectivist, the basis of faith and relationship with God are the facts of history, the facts of reality. To the subjectivist, the basis of faith and relationship with God is the experience of the Divine. Evangelical Christianity claims to be both objectivist and subjectivist, for both aspects are necessary. It is not sufficient that there is simply an objective reality in which we have our faith, nor is it right that we have faith in some ethereal being of our own making.

For an example of total subjectivism we need look no farther than Alcoholics Anonymous. It doesn't matter what you believe, provided that you believe that there is a power greater than yourself. The power greater than yourself does not have to have an existence that is knowable in any way, but you must be willing to experience it.

Many people, of course, are precisely the opposite—they believe that God exists and that Jesus rose from the dead, but have no direct relationship with him. How do we combine the objective facts of the death and resurrection of Jesus with our subjective experience?

Repentance and Faith

Jesus pronounced the coming of the Kingdom of God and called people to repent and believe the gospel.[2] John the Baptist made the same challenge to repentance.[3] Throughout John's gospel we find Jesus challenging people to put their faith in the

[2] Mark 1:14f; Matt 4:17
[3] Matt 3:2; Mark 1:4

[1] Acts 2:38; 17:30; 16:31

[4] Acts 20:21

Son of God. When the disciples first preached the gospel they called upon people to repent and believe.[1] Paul can summarise his ministry as declaring "to both Jews and Greeks that they must turn to God in repentance and have faith in our Lord Jesus".[2]

We will see in due course that this repentance and faith are the bricks and mortar of the bridge between the first and twentieth centuries. Let's look at them in more detail.

1. Repentance

[3] 1 Thess 1:9,10
[4] Acts 20:21; 16:30

Repentance is turning oneself away from a present pattern of life, to a new way of living. It is a change of mind which flows through into a changed attitude and behaviour. It need not be a specifically religious idea, although for Christians it obviously will be—it is God to whom we are turning. A classic expression of repentance is the Thessalonian experience of turning to God from idols[3], but the gospel goes to all people as a challenge to repent: "Turn to God".[4]

2. Faith

[5] James 2:14-26
[6] James 2:19

Faith is firmness and commitment. Faith is to rely on, or depend on, or trust somebody or something, or some message. It involves intellectual assent that the thing is true, but more importantly, it is an expression of something's trustworthiness. It can be used to mean bare belief, that is, the acknowledgement that something is true, but by itself such belief is dead and useless[5]. This is the 'belief' of the demons.[6] Real Christian faith is to act upon what we believe to be true—to rely upon it, to trust, depend and commit ourselves to it.

[7] Luke 17:10

[8] Galatians 2:21
[9] John 14:6

The alternatives to repentance and faith are pride and merit. Faith requires me to renounce self-sufficiency and to become a dependant. Faith is therefore always antithetical to pride. Repentance likewise, calls upon me to turn away from self-determination in order to put my trust in God.

Furthermore, in both faith and repentance, there is a denial of any merit on our part. We are not saved by works, but by Jesus Christ. The works that we do are never sufficient to bring us credit before God[7]. More significantly, if meritorious works could bring us salvation, God's self sacrifice in the death of his Son would be unnecessary[8]. It is only through the death of Jesus that we can enter the presence of God[9]. Faith in Jesus is a denial of faith in our merit. We may choose to put our faith in our good works, or in Jesus, but we cannot have it both ways.

Misunderstanding Repentance and Faith

Justification by faith alone is fundamental to our understanding of the gospel. This was the great battle cry of the Reformation. In discovering this, Luther saw the gates of heaven opened before him, for he saw that righteousness is something that comes from God and is declared to us in the death of Jesus, rather than something that comes from us and is earned by our merit.

However, if repentance and faith are our responses to God, are we not being saved by making the right responses? Instead of having many works of obedience, have we now got two works of obedience—repentance and faith? If we are saved by our faith, are we not contributing faith to the death of Jesus and so still saving ourselves?

The New Testament is insistent that salvation is a free gift of God. In Ephesians 2:8,9, we are told explicitly: "For it is by grace you have been saved, through faith—and this is not from yourselves, it is the gift of God—not by works, so that no-one can boast". The word 'this' refers to the whole activity of salvation, not to the faith through which we have been saved. We have nothing of which we can boast in our salvation. We are God's workmanship, created in Christ Jesus.[1]

[1] Ephesians 2:10

Viewing repentance and faith as meritorious acts has provided some people with an **alternative** to faith in the death of Jesus, and for other people an **addition** to the death of Jesus. In the first category are the Muslims, who find it very difficult to see any need for an atoning sacrifice: Why doesn't God just forgive the repentant?[2] More common among Christians is the idea that we can add our faith and repentance to the death of Jesus. This always implies that the death of Jesus is in some way inadequate.

[2] However, Muslims do preactice sacrifice for certain sins

Seeing repentance and faith as meritorious acts also fails to do justice to the doctrine of sinfulness. We have seen previously in these studies that in our sinfulness we are dead[3] and blind[4] and ignorant.[5] The slaves of sin are controlled by the sinful nature and therefore cannot please God.[6] Even though Jesus invites people to come to him, he knows that "no one can come to me unless the Father who sent me draws him".[7]

[3] Ephesians 2:3
[4] 2 Cor 4:4
[5] 1 Cor 2:14
[6] Rom 8:8; John 8:34
[7] John 6:44, 65

We 'appropriate' (or take to ourselves) the death of Jesus by repentance and faith. The gospel commands this of us. This repentance and faith doesn't add in any way to the death of Jesus, nor bring us any merit or credit. And given our sinfulness, such repentance and faith cannot come from ourselves. If it could, there might be some grounds for boasting and some means of salvation other than faith in the Lord Jesus. How then can we repent and put our faith in the death of Jesus for salvation?

The Promised Work Of The Spirit

[1] Jer 31:31ff

[2] Joel 2:28ff

[3] Ezek 36:24-28

In the Old Testament, the prophets speak of a new age when God will write a new covenant on the hearts of his people.[1] Forgiveness of sins is to be part of this new age, and so is the pouring out of God's Spirit. The Spirit that the prophets enjoyed will be shared by all who are in the covenant people of God.[2] The Spirit will be poured into the hearts of God's washed people so that they will be moved to obey and follow his laws and his words.[3]

Research

Study Acts 2:14-41.

How does Pentecost fulfil the Old Testament expectation?

Which person of the Trinity is the focus of Peter's 'Pentecostal' sermon?

How is the outpouring of the Spirit related to Jesus' identity (cf. Romans 1:4)?

Jesus promised the coming of the Spirit who would guide and guard the disciples and would "convict the world of guilt in regard to sin and righteousness and judgement".[1] In the resurrection and ascension of Jesus we have received what he (and his Father) promised, that the gospel may be believed and preached, winning repentance and forgiveness of sins.[2]

[1] John 16:8

[2] Luke 24:45-49; Acts 1:8

Through this outpouring of the Spirit we come to new birth. We have been looking forward to the "renewal of all things when the Son of Man sits on his glorious throne"[3] and we experience the beginning of that renewal when the Spirit comes into our life, regenerating us.[4]

[3] Matthew 19:28

[4] Titus 3:5

This new birth enables us to turn back in repentance and faith. We are not born by our own desires, will or strength, but by the grace of God.[5] It is the anointing of the Holy Spirit that teaches us the truth of the gospel,[6] so that everyone who believes that Jesus is the Christ is born of God.[7] We must get this in the right order—it is the rebirth that inevitably leads to belief in Jesus, not the belief in Jesus that leads to the rebirth, for then we would be giving ourselves birth! Just as no-one can come to the Son unless the Father draws him,[8] so also "all that the Father gives me will come to me".[9] Just as we were blinded by the god of this world, so that we could not see the light of the gospel, so it is God that has said, "Let light shine out of darkness", and has made light to shine in our hearts to give us the knowledge of the glory of God in the face of Christ.[10]

[5] John 1:12,13
[6] 1 John 2:20,27
[7] 1 John 5:1

[8] John 6:44
[9] John 6:37

[10] 2 Corinthians 4:4-6

As a result of God's Spirit overcoming our sinful rejection of the gospel, **both faith and repentance are to be seen as a gift of God.** In the book of Acts we see Christians in Jerusalem concluding that "God has granted even the Gentiles repentance unto life".[11] Luke later records about the Gentiles that "all who were appointed for eternal life believed".[12] He also describes the conversion of Lydia by saying "the Lord opened her heart to respond to Paul's message".[13] So the response to the gospel, both in repentance and faith, is the gift of God.

[11] Acts 11:18
[12] Acts 13:48

[13] Acts 16:14

The Spirit's sovereignty in regenerating us prior to conversion leads inevitably to the doctrine of predestination—as the book of Acts says "all who were appointed for eternal life believed".[14] Only some will respond to the invitation to all men—those regenerated by God's sovereign will.

[14] Acts 13:48

Misunderstanding The Work Of The Spirit

The nature of the death of Jesus as a full, sufficient sacrifice for sins; the incapacitating effects of our sinfulness; the character of faith and repentance; and the impossibility of merit—all these mean that conversion cannot take place before regeneration. It is the Spirit's work of awakening us and regenerating us which leads to our conversion—our repentance and faith. But how does this take place? Can we bring it about ourselves?

Nicodemus was warned that the Spirit is like the wind, moving wherever he wishes and without human control. However, man has often tried to tame the wind and he does likewise with the Spirit. Some have tried to do it through sacraments, hoping to force the Spirit to bless those whom we bless. But there is no promise from God that our sacramental actions bind him to work according to our will. The Spirit is sovereign and he will work as he chooses.

Others try to channel the work of the Spirit by the laying on of hands, or by 'waiting' or 'being open'. If we adopt these various techniques, they say, God's Spirit will invariably descend. This is simply another example of seeking to move the Spirit where we wish.

In the Bible, the Spirit accompanies the preaching of the word of God. He takes the seed of the gospel message and from it brings new life. He does not do this invariably with all preaching of the gospel, but it is his chosen method of operation. We need to accept this and abandon other methods, no matter how fashionable they may be.

Crossing The Bridge

Understanding how the objective facts of history are applied subjectively affects the way in which we minister the gospel. It is not an intellectual activity that we are engaged in, but a spiritual warfare. We must pray to God for his Spirit to work in the hearts and minds of people, for it is only as his Spirit opens their eyes that they can hear and understand the gospel. Likewise we must be faithful to the gospel message and not seek to tailor it to modern opinion. It is our job to convey the objective truth; it is the work of God's Spirit that will bring it to subjective conviction.

Just as all this affects the way we minister, so it will also affect the way we live as Christians. There can be no boasting, credit, arrogance or pride in our stand as Christians. It is all of grace. Therefore we have "complete faith" for we depend totally upon him for our salvation. Anybody, irrespective of how degenerate or religious or moral they might be, can come on equal terms to the throne of God. Consequently, we can be united with each other on a profound level, for the things of human distinctiveness and credit are irrelevant before the judgement seat of God.

We are truly one in Christ Jesus.

This teaching of the Scriptures on how we appropriate the death of Jesus is stated in the seventh statement of the AFES doctrinal basis:

The necessity of the work of the Holy Spirit to make the death of Christ effective in the individual sinner, granting him repentance toward God and faith in Jesus Christ.

Think it through

1   Summarise what the Bible means by:

'repentance'

'faith'

2   Why is the Spirit's work a **necessity** in us appropriating the death of Christ?

3   "The Spirit's sovereignty in regenerating us prior to conversion leads inevitably to the doctrine of predestination." How do you react to this statement? What effect will this understanding of conversion have on evangelism?

Other notes

8

What — no controversy?

Doctrinal Basis and Controversy

Most doctrinal statements are written in the context of controversy. The Creeds of the ancient church specifically and explicitly ruled out alternatives to genuine Christianity.[1] The great Reformation and Puritan creeds pointedly rejected the errors of medievalism.[2] Similarly, the doctrinal basis of the International Fellowship of Evangelical Students (IFES) was written to expound Evangelicalism in a manner that would exclude non-Evangelicalism. The prominence given to the inspiration and infallibility of Scripture, the seriousness with which sin is taken, the importance of a substitutionary view of the atonement, and the necessity of the regenerating work of the Holy Spirit, clearly indicate the distinctive character of Evangelical faith. These doctrines carefully exclude the alternatives to Evangelical faith, such as Liberalism and Roman Catholicism. They are as distinctive as the Reformation doctrines of grace alone, Scripture alone, and faith alone.

However, doctrinal statements also include basic teachings about the gospel. They are not wholly negative, simply pointing out the errors of alternative doctrines—they also seek to be positive. Some of the doctrinal statements of the IFES speak of the Trinity, or the resurrection of Jesus from the dead, in a way that the vast majority of non-Evangelicals would be happy to endorse. One such non-controversial statement of the AFES doctrinal basis concerns the work of the Holy Spirit. The eighth of the statements reads:

The indwelling and work of the Holy Spirit in the believer.

It is hard to imagine a Christian tradition which would deny this statement. Theoretically all Christians would subscribe to the indwelling and work of the Holy Spirit in the believer.

Effectively, however, many have denied it, both from a Liberal and Catholic perspective. The Liberal commitment to rationality and the mind has left little room for work of the Holy

[1] The Apostles', Nicene and Athanasian Creeds

[2] The Confessions of Augsberg (1530) and Geneva (1536), the Belgic Confession (1561), the 39 Articles (1563), the Westminster Confession (1646)

71

Spirit in the life of the believer. The Catholic insistence on the authority of the church has also diminished the authority of the Holy Spirit in the individual believer.

Grounds for controversy

Disagreement in this area has been over the *manner* and *nature* of this indwelling and work of the Holy Spirit in the believer. As this work has played very little part in Catholic or Liberal theology, there has not been a great exposition of the Spirit's work to which the Evangelical must reply. However, since the writing of the doctrinal basis, considerable controversy has arisen through the Charismatic and neo-Pentecostal movements. These theological disagreements are not new—they are centuries old—but they have been given new prominence in Evangelical circles of recent years. Do we need to revise our doctrinal statements?

Good doctrinal statements exclude the erroneous and the irrelevant. There is a tendency for those of us committed to a doctrinal position to try to say more than the Scriptures are saying. We try to tack down every last area of disagreement so that total certainty can be established. This was the problem of the church at Ephesus—they were strong in seeing false apostles and false teachers but weak in maintaining their first love.[1] The Scriptures encourage us to welcome the weak brother and not engage him in disputes.[2] Nit-picking arguments, disagreements about genealogies and the like, are also seen as ungodly.[3]

[1] Rev 2:2-4

[2] Romans 14

[3] 2 Tim 2:14-16; 23-24

The Bible does speak of the work of the Holy Spirit in the life of the Christian. However, our knowledge of **all** that the Bible says, and our understanding about **how** the Holy Spirit works in our lives, are not essential beliefs to qualify as a Christian. This is an area in which Christians may still be in disagreement, yet retain their common faith in the Lord Jesus Christ. If we did not believe in the indwelling work of the Holy Spirit, then, like the people whom Paul met in Ephesus, we would need to have the gospel properly explained to us.[4] But if we do believe in the indwelling work of the Holy Spirit, then the essential spiritual element of the work of the gospel is agreed upon.

[4] Acts 19:1-7

This does not mean that we cannot be in serious error through our particular view of the indwelling and work of the Holy Spirit. It is possible to put such emphasis upon the work of the Spirit that we effectively deny the other doctrinal statements that have already been covered in this series. Some imply that because of the work of the Spirit in their lives, they do not need the atoning redemption of the death of Jesus. Such a belief is totally inconsistent with what is meant in the doctrinal basis by believing in the indwelling and work of the Holy Spirit in the believer. Others believe that the Spirit has come in a new and different fashion from the day of Pentecost, working through some modern prophet who adds to the message of Jesus Christ. Again this will effectively undermine the whole doctrinal basis.

If we are to understand this statement of the doctrinal basis we must do it in the light of its context—that is, the total theological viewpoint spelt out in the eleven statements. It may be frustrating that our modern controversies are not being directly addressed, but it is important that we affirm the reality of the work of the Spirit in our lives. Sometimes, in entering into controversy, we lose perspective on the subject at hand. We are too ready to make it into a gospel issue and exclude our opponents. Sometimes we allow the agenda of the doctrinal statement to be set by our opponents, rather than by the word of God. And sometimes we withdraw from affirming the work of the Spirit in reaction to those who never talk about anything else.

In today's Evangelical world, this statement in the doctrinal basis is possibly the most controversial. However, it is expressed in the least controversial terms! All sides would ascribe to the sentiments of this statement. We must turn to what the Scriptures say about the indwelling and work of the Holy Spirit and see how this is consistent with the total doctrinal position of the AFES doctrinal basis. In so doing, we might make some contribution to the debate and give some doctrinal guidance for our continuing unity and fellowship.

The Indwelling Of The Holy Spirit

The doctrinal basis has already stated its belief in "The presence and power of the Holy Spirit in the work of regeneration" . That is, evangelical belief is committed to a spiritual perception of the gospel and doctrine. Christianity is not a set of dry propositions, unrelated to spiritual transformation; not a set of ideas, but a living faith. Without the work of the Holy Spirit in the lives of individuals, no-one would respond to the gospel message.

However, the Spirit's work does not stop at the point of regeneration. The Spirit does not lead us to the new birth and then leave us to grow alone. The New Testament is committed to the idea of the ongoing, indwelling of the Holy Spirit in the believer. The believer's life is not to be a cleansed and empty house awaiting the return of evil, but a regenerated heart now continually indwelt by God's Holy Spirit.[1]

[1] Luke 11:24-26

73

Research

Look at the following passages and list what they tell us about the indwelling of the Holy Spirit in the believer.

1 John 2:24-27

Ephesians 1:13-14 (cf. 2 Corinthians 5:15)

Romans 8:12-17 (cf. Galatians 4:17)

2 Corinthians 6:16 (cf. 1 Corinthians 6:19)

Without the doctrine of the indwelling of the Holy Spirit, Christianity would be a mere credence, or association. People believe in many things from socialism to Rugby Union, but Christianity is not just another thing to believe in. To be Christian is to be in a living relationship with the creator of the universe as our Father and to have his very presence, in the person of the Holy Spirit, dwelling within us.

The Work Of The Holy Spirit In Believers

The Old Testament promises the coming of the Holy Spirit. When the law of God was given to Israel on the mountain, they responded in obedient faith and God declared "I have heard what this people said to you. Everything they said was good. O, that their hearts would be inclined to fear me and keep all my commands always, so that it might go well with them and their children forever!"[1] Israel's obedience was shortlived, however, for though they had the commands of God written on tables of stone, their hearts did not follow the law of God. God's promise was for a new covenant where the same law would be re-written, not on tables of stone, but on human hearts.[2] God would be their teacher.[3] He would place his Spirit within them to move them

[1] Deut 5:28-29

[2] Jer 31:31-34
[3] Isaiah 54:13

74

to obey his commands.[1] The Spirit of God would be poured out, not just on the kings or the prophets, but upon all God's people.[2]

These great promises are fulfilled on the day of Pentecost when the risen Christ pours out his Spirit upon his people.[3] Now, as Christians give testimony to Jesus, they fulfil their Spirit-given role of prophecy.[4] The Christian has the mind of Christ, for the Spirit has revealed to him the truths that were hidden for generations.[5] It is this anointing of the Spirit that teaches us God's word so that we no longer need authoritative teachers or interpreters.[6] The vicar of Christ on earth is the Holy Spirit, who dwells in the heart of each Christian person, teaching them his word and moving them to obey it.

From Pentecost onwards, Christians are those who have been baptised by the Spirit. The Spirit floods into us, regenerating us, and teaching us that Jesus is Lord,[7] that God is our Father,[8] and that we are God's people, assured of his future.[9] And with the coming of the Spirit into our life, God's word works in us,[10] producing a crop of love, joy, peace, patience, kindness, goodness, faithfulness, gentleness and self-control.[11] The Spirit is now leading us to put to death the misdeeds of the body and to wage war against the 'flesh' (or the 'sinful nature', as the NIV translates it).[12] This is being led, or carried along by, the Spirit of God. It is worth noting that the phrase "led by the Spirit" is used only twice in the New Testament and on both occasions it highlights the primary work of the Spirit in the life of the Christian, namely to turn away from sin to a new life of obedience in Jesus. We must not understate or gloss over this dynamic, miraculous activity of the Spirit in the lives of Christians—we who were once powerless to please or obey God are now being transformed into his very likeness.[13]

Moreover, the Spirit ensures that this process comes to consummation. Not only is his very presence a deposit or guarantee of the future, but he helps us in our weakness. Faced with the sufferings of this world, and with the temptation to lose faith in God's power and goodness to save us, it is the Spirit who intercedes for us with groans that words cannot express.[14]

However, our preservation and edification as Christians also involves our corporate life. As we grow like Christ, we should expect to be concerned for other people's salvation. As Christ gives his Spirit to us, we must demonstrate or manifest his Spirit in serving others for their salvation. These spiritual gifts are called the gifts of Christ and the gifts of God, but not 'the gifts of the Spirit'—they are manifestations of the Spirit that the Father and Son have given us.[15] They are given for the **common** good, that is, for our mutual up-building in Christlikeness. As diverse

[1] Ezekiel 36:26-28; 37:24-28

[2] Joel 2:28-32; Numbers 11:29

[3] Acts 2:14-36

[4] Revelation 1:2,9; 20:10

[5] 1 Corinthians 2:10-16

[6] 1 John 2:24-27

[7] 1 Corinthians 12:3; John 16:8-11

[8] Romans 8:12-16; Galatians 4:1-7

[9] Ephesians 1:13-14; 2 Corinthians 5:5

[10] 1 Thessalonians 2:13; Hebrews 4:12-13

[11] Galatians 5:22-23

[12] Romans 8:12-14; Galatians 5:16-18

[13] 2 Cor 3:17-18

[14] Romans 8:23, 26-27

[15] Romans 12:3-8; 1 Corinthians 12:7

[1] 1 Corinthians 13   manifestations of the same Spirit, they are to be used in accordance with the fruit of the Spirit, particularly in love.[1]

Christians must therefore go on being filled with the Spirit for the common good. As we are filled with the Spirit we will speak to one another and submit to one another as we sing and give thanks to God the Father for everything in the name of our

[2] Ephesians 5:19-21   Lord Jesus Christ.[2]

To summarise: the New Testament does not discuss the method and mechanism by which the Spirit works so much as his aim and direction. He works because Jesus has died and

[3] John 14-16; 7:38-39   risen and poured him into our hearts.[3] He is the deposit and assurance from God of our eternal salvation, being the first part of the heavenly reality. His work within Christians is the application of the gospel to our lives. Just as he brought us to new birth through the gospel of Jesus, so he carries on that work in transforming us into the likeness of Christ. He teaches us that God is our Father, and that Jesus is our Lord. He maintains our relationship with God in prayer. And he produces the fruit of holiness in our lives, working through us for other people's salvation and edification.

So Where's The Controversy?

The indwelling and work of the Holy Spirit has been taught by the Scriptures and Bible-believing Christians down the centuries. The Holy Spirit has never been 'the forgotten Person of the Trinity'. In every generation, new writings on the work of the Holy Spirit have been published by Christians. All who have faith in Jesus as their Lord and know God as their Father have experienced the work of the Holy Spirit in their lives, transforming them into the image of Christ himself.

Yet repeatedly through the centuries, people have come to new and different understandings of the work of the Spirit. These teachings have varied from one fad and fashion to another. However, they all detach the work of the Spirit from the gospel. The work of the Spirit becomes something that runs parallel to, but does not derive from, or lead to, the work of Christ. A wedge is driven between the work of the Spirit and the word of God, which is the Spirit's sword. Christians are encouraged to find an experience of the gospel in addition to, and separate from, the experience of Christ. The gifts of Christ are called the 'gifts of the Spirit' and the church of Christ called the 'Spirit-filled church'. The idolatrous religious bric-a-brac industry replaces the cross of Christ with the dove of the Spirit.

The eighth article of the AFES doctrinal basis does not

address these controversies. It simply proclaims our firm belief in the indwelling and work of the Spirit in the life of the believer. In light of the Bible's emphasis, and the way it defines the Spirit's indwelling and work, we would do well to reaffirm this important teaching. And the present climate, with its emphasis on how the Spirit works, makes this affirmation all the more imperative.

Think it through

1   What is the primary work of the Holy Spirit in believers?

2   What does it mean to be "led by the Spirit"?

3   In what ways have you experienced a different emphasis from the Bible's regarding the work of the Spirit?

4   If the Spirit indwells us, in what sense does Christ "live in us"? (cf. Galatians 2:20 and John 14:5-27)

5   What aspects of the Spirit's work are essential for Christians to believe? How will this affect our unity and fellowship?

Other notes

9

Godly heresies

Many heresies come from godly desires.

Universalism, for example, teaches that all mankind will be saved. The Bible, on the other hand, speaks of hell and punishment, and of many being on the road to destruction. How can Bible-believers arrive at Universalism? By godly desires. God does not desire the death of a sinner, and there will be joy in heaven over any sinner who repents.[1] We must not find joy, therefore, in the death and punishment of the wicked, but rather joy in their repentance and life. Our desire must be that all people will be saved—this is a godly desire. However, it is not the plan of God.

[1] Ezek 18:31-32; Luke 15:7,10,31f

We do not always understand why God's **desires** and God's **plans** are not identical. We sometimes get confused over the 'will' of God. The word 'will' can refer to his desire/wish, or his plan. That is, if you ask "Was it the will of God for Jesus to die?" the answer is both yes and no. If you mean, "Was it his **wish** that an innocent man be murdered?" the answer must be no. But if you mean, "Was it his **plan** that Jesus be crucified?" the answer must be yes. We are not always able to understand how and why his plans differ from his desires, but it is clearly revealed in Scripture that they do. So while it is godly to *desire* that all people saved, we must not allow that godly desire to push us into the heresy that all men *will* be saved.

Four godly desires

The sicknesses and sufferings of this world, especially those that lead to death, are part of the judgement of God on our fallen world. God's ultimate goal is the creation of a new heavens and a new earth where there will no longer be any pain and suffering, sickness, death or mourning.[2] Jesus was filled with compassion for the sick and healed them. It is godly to desire that sickness and death be done away with forever.

Healing

[2] Revelation 21:3-4

Justice   Jesus taught us to pray for God's will to be done on earth as it is in heaven. God had made known his will on earth in the old covenant through the Law, which reflected his concern for justice and righteousness. Isaiah prophesied about the Messiah: "Of the increase of his government and peace there will be no end. He will reign on David's throne and over his Kingdom establishing and upholding it with justice and righteousness from that time on and for ever".[1] It is a godly desire to look for a world in which justice reigns, where the widow and the fatherless are not oppressed. It is right to want economic and political justice.

[1] Isaiah 9:7

Perfection   "You must be perfect as your Father in heaven is perfect," Jesus taught his disciples.[2] Pursuing the holiness and perfection of God should dominate our lives.[3] Christ has died to take away the sins of many people and no one who is born of God will continue to sin because God's seed remains in him.[4] Indeed, the Epistle of John is written in order that we will not sin.[5] Yes, it is a godly desire to have done with sin. We must hate even the clothing that is stained by corrupted flesh.[6]

[2] Matthew 5:48
[3] 1 Peter 1:15-16
[4] Heb 9:28; 1 John 3:9
[5] 1 John 2:1
[6] Jude 23

Prosperity   Under the old covenant, God repeatedly promised material prosperity for his obedient people. The classic statement of this is in Deuteronomy 28, where God's pleasure at Israel's obedience and his hatred of their rebellion are reflected in a set of blessings and curses. If Israel obeys God they will be blessed in the city and in the country, in their families, in their commerce, in their crops and livestock—in every conceivable aspect of life. Throughout the Bible, God is portrayed as the giver of riches and all good things of life. And it is right to enjoy the blessings he showers on his people.

The Heresy

However, the great heresy associated with each of these godly desires is the expectation of their fulfilment in this world, rather than the age to come. While it is true that with the death and resurrection of Jesus, the Kingdom of God was established, and that we now participate in it through his Spirit, the Kingdom of God has not yet reached its consummation. The New Testament looks forward to the return of the Lord Jesus Christ when everything will be placed under his feet and when all the benefits of the kingdom will be ours in their fulness.[7]

[7] Revelation 21-22

This belief in the personal return of the Lord Jesus is captured in the final statement of the Australian Fellowship of Evangelical Students' (AFES) doctrinal basis:

The expectation of the personal return of the Lord Jesus Christ.

This doctrinal statement must not only be believed as a statement of Christian truth, but also allowed to influence our thinking about the present reality of Christianity and our future hope. That is, today there are many people who would tick the box next to the eleventh statement of the basis, saying that they did believe in the personal return of the Lord Jesus Christ. Yet these people have no place for the return of the Lord Jesus Christ in their thinking about the world. Consequently, the things that are promised to accompany the return of the Lord Jesus Christ, such as healing, justice, perfection and prosperity, are attributed to the present, rather than the future. In this way, the Biblical doctrine of expectation, or 'hope', is seriously distorted and the pattern of Christian living is disfigured.

Conversely, there are some people who literally deny the personal return of the Lord Jesus Christ. Such people usually also deny the divinity of Christ and his resurrection from the dead. Their Christianity is either barren of all spiritual, supernatural elements, or else has turned into an anti-creationist, Platonic, Eastern-style mysticism. The bodily resurrection of Jesus and his personal return are repugnant to their spiritual sensibilities.

The Bible and the personal return

The Bible frequently speaks of the personal return of the Lord Jesus Christ. At his ascension, Jesus promises to return in the same way he left, and the rest of the New Testament is unanimous in looking forward to this future, space-time event.[1] Moreover, Christians are frequently described in terms of their attitude to this event. We, like the Thessalonians, are 'waiters'.[2] Our attitude of heavenly-mindedness, of having our hearts set on the manifestation of Jesus in all his glory, should contrast sharply with the non-Christian preoccupation with this world.

By the end of the New Testament period, some people were doubting the return of the Lord Jesus. The apostle Peter gives a firm answer to those who would scoff, assuring us of a day of judgement (as certainly as the world was created by a word and destroyed by a word in the flood).[3] The day of the Lord will come suddenly and unexpectedly like a thief in the night. The delay is only for the sake of people to repent that they may be saved.

[1] Among many others see Acts 1:11; 1 Cor 15:23; Heb 10:28; Titus 2:13
[2] 1 Thess 1:9-10
[3] 2 Peter 3

[1] 1 Thess 1:9-10; Rom 5:9-10; Heb 9:28

[2] 1 Thess 1:7-9; 2 Cor 5:10

[3] 2 Thess 1:7-10; Phil 3:20f; 1 Cor 15:23,50-57; Col 3:4; 1 John 3:2

[4] 2 Peter 3:1-13

[5] Revelation 19-22

[6] 1 Cor 15:23-28; John 14:3

[7] There are a number of different theories concerning the nature of the millenium—the thousand year reign of Christ mentioned in Revelation 20.

[7] 1 Thess 5:8; Titus 3:7

When Christ returns he will rescue his people from the wrath of God.[1] He will come in judgement and we will all sit before his judgement seat.[2] However, for the Christians, he comes to be glorified by us and to glorify us, transforming us into his likeness.[3]

This return of Jesus is not just a personal event for Christians when they die, but is of cosmic proportions. This world will be done away with and a new heavens and new earth created.[4] The great wedding feast of the Lamb will take place.[5] It has personal implications in that Christ will take us to be with him, but it is more than this—it involves the end of all things and the beginning of a whole new created order.[6]

The doctrinal statement is wisely silent about millennial speculations.[7] Christian believers have been divided down the centuries by different millennial views. This should not be an issue over which Christians break fellowship. The New Testament warns against speculating about the time of the coming of the Lord. Instead, we must always be prepared, for he will come unexpectedly and unmistakably. Then it will be too late to repent and put matters right—the end will have come.

Living in light of the coming

So what should be the nature of life now, this side of the second coming? The key New Testament word is 'hope' or 'expectation'. We have the hope of salvation, the hope of eternal life.[8] We rejoice and boast in the hope of the glory of God.

[8] Rom 5:2; Heb 3:6;10:23

[9] Romans 8:24

[10] Heb 11; Phil 3:12-21

The essence of hope lies in non-possession. As Paul asks rhetorically, "Who hopes for what he already has?"[9] Christians are living in pilgrimage, dissatisfied with this world and looking forward to the one that lies ahead.[10]

Research

The New Testament has much to say about our hope for the world to come and how it should affect our lives. Note down what the following references reveal.

Philippians 3:12-14

Philippians 3:20-21

2 Peter 3:7-13

Romans 5:2-5

Romans 8:18-25

Colossians 3:1-4

The importance of true doctrine

Truth is truth and should be valued as such. But truth is indivisible—each part of the truth contributes to every other part. Denying or misunderstanding the truth in one particular area affects our perception of truth in many other areas.

The personal return of the Lord Jesus is clearly taught in Scripture, and believing this truth affects many other aspects of our belief. This truth holds in balance our understanding of the world today as well as our hope for the future. While it continues to be godly to desire health, justice, holiness, and prosperity, our expectation is that only in the return of the Lord Jesus Christ will these things be ours fully.

The sufferings of this present age produce in us optimism and hope for the future. They take our eyes and minds off this world and point them to the next. While it may be godly to desire the removal of these evils now, that godly desire must find its expression in the prayer "Come, Lord Jesus". The present delay is for the nations to repent. It gives us the opportunity to preach the gospel that others may know the saving grace of God, that others may share in the hope of glory. Even now we know that God is at work in everything to bring us to that glory.[1] Thus we can joyfully endure the sufferings of this age, knowing that they are not to be compared with the glory that is to be revealed.[2]

This loss of this perspective has lead many Christians down the sidetracks of the 'social gospel', the healing ministry, the perfectionist movement and the prosperity doctrine. These distort the gospel of Jesus, and deceive their members, by offering now what can only be received in the future.

We must remain committed to the expectation, and the implications, of the personal return of the Lord Jesus.

[1] Rom 8:28-30

[2] James 1:3-5; Rom 8:17ff; 5:2-5

Think it through

1   What is the key Christian response to the approaching return of Christ? How will this be worked out in our lives?

2   What do we know about the time and manner of Christ's return?

3   What should our attitude be to things like healing, justice, perfection and prosperity?

4   Are Christians basically optimists or pessimists about our world?

Other notes

Appendix
Who is in control?

For the atheist, standing alone on his hill, the world spread out below him is under no-one's control. There is no great Architect, let alone a great Executive Director. He can accept, therefore, with pessimism the irrationality, hostility and absurdity that he sees. Alternatively, he can take upon himself the responsibility of trying to run the world.

Most people, even atheists, realise that they cannot personally run the world. However, some feel that by corporate endeavour, humanity can and will bring the world under control. This belies the facts. Humanity has tremendous trouble ruling itself, especially when trying to work out which part of humanity should do the ruling. The atheist is caught between an unrealistic optimism (expressed in the Humanist Party) and a bewildering and unlivable pessimism (expressed in Existentialism).

By itself this is not sufficient reason to believe in God. However, belief in God does remove us from the terrible tensions of atheism, provided, that is, we believe in the God who is **sovereign**. Belief in the sovereign God gives us purpose and meaning, values and direction. Life is not a random string of meaningless events. Life is, as we perceive it to be, purposeful and significant.

However, some believers in God do not believe in a thoroughly sovereign God. They may be dualists who think of two gods, one good and one evil, constantly at war with each other—and never certain of the outcome. Or they perceive a god who is weak and ineffectual, constantly waiting for man to do the right thing. Such a weak and ineffectual god is man's servant, rather than his master. Man, in this schema, is the real god, and 'God' has become his lackey. Others cannot understand how a truly sovereign God can allow a world which is so full of evil, or a world where man seems to be able to express his freedom.

The Evangelical position is expressed in the following doctrinal statement:[1]

The Sovereignty of God in creation, revelation, redemption and final judgement.

[1] This statement is not included in the AFES Doctrinal Basis, but does appear in the Doctrinal Basis of the IFES, the international student group with which AFES is affiliated. It is such a helpful and instructive statement that we thought it worth including as an appendix

87

The word 'sovereignty' means kingly rule or supreme power. Most modern monarchs have very limited power, and so to speak of God as 'king' is to represent him as some kind of figurehead, fondly regarded but with no real power. Within the Scriptures God is constantly portrayed as the king who rules the universe in all power and might and strength. It is this **Lordship** of God which the second article of Evangelical belief affirms.

God is the ruler in all the affairs of life: creation, revelation, redemption, and final judgement. The rest of the doctrinal basis spells out the sovereignty of God in these various areas and, in one sense, this statement is unnecessary. The other statements make clear how he is the ruler in redemption, revelation and judgement (although not much more is said of his sovereignty in creation). However, this article acts as a helpful summary, and emphasises the notion of his **sovereignty**, rather than explaining how he operates in these various areas. To understand this article correctly, we need to understand the other doctrinal articles as well, and we will come to each of them in due course.

Research

Study Ephesians 1:1-14 and note down what it teaches about God's sovereignty.

God is sovereign in creation

From the beginning to the end of the Bible, God is known as the creator. The first chapter of the Bible speaks of his sovereign establishment of the universe in its place. As Psalm 33:6 says "By the word of the LORD were the heavens made, their starry host by the breath of his mouth". God is always known as one who has made everything, even from nothing. The LORD says "Heaven is my throne, the earth is my footstool. Where is the house you will build for me? Where will my resting place be? Has not my hand made all these things, and so they came into being?".[1]

[1] Isa 66:1,2.

God is worthy to receive all glory, honour and power "for you created all things, and by your will they were created and have their being".[2] All things were created by God for his plan and purpose. They are viewed by him as being good. Even in the fallen state, "everything God created is good, and nothing is to be rejected if it is received with thanksgiving, because it is consecrated by the word of God and prayer".[3] God did not create chaos, nor something empty, but rather "he who created the heavens, he is God; he who fashioned and made the earth, he founded it; he did not create it to be empty, but formed it to be inhabited".[4] Mankind is part of God's good creation. We have our being and existence in God, just as the rest of the world around us exists because of his will and purpose.[5] It was God's intention that man, of all creation, should be created in his image.

[2] Revelation 4:11

[3] 1 Timothy 4:4-5

[4] Isa 45:18

[5] Acts 17:24-28

While creation is frequently ascribed to God the Father, each of the three persons of the Trinity were engaged in creation. Not very much is said of the work of the Spirit in creation. He is said to be hovering over the waters in the second verse of the Bible, but he is not often related to the work of creation. However, the Son frequently is. We are told that all things were made through him and "without him nothing was made that has been made".[6] "By him all things were created: things in heaven and on earth, visible and invisible, whether thrones or powers or rulers or authorities; all things were created by him and for him. He is before all things, and in him all things hold together." Therefore, he is known as the firstborn of all creation.[7]

[6] John 1:3

[7] Col 1:16f; cf. Heb 1:2f; 1 Cor 8:6

God's sovereignty in creation goes beyond the initial 'making of everything'. Because everything is made in accordance with his plan, he continues to sustain, uphold and control the created universe. The deistic notion of the clock maker who has made a machine that runs of its own accord is inconsistent with

[1] Matt 10:29-30

the Bible's view of God. He has every hair of our head numbered and no sparrow falls to the ground unobserved.[1]

Yet God is not to be confused with the created world. He existed prior to creation. He is over and above the creation and must not be represented by anything in creation. Pantheism, which confuses the creation and the creator, is inconsistent with the Scriptures. God is sovereign in creation.

God is sovereign in revelation

In a society dominated by 'rationality', God is often sought through the deductive process. The traditional proofs for the existence of God—the argument from contingency, from teleology, ontology and so on—have often been used by Christians as a rational defence for the knowledge of God. Man, by his thinking processes, has been able to discover 'god'.

[2] Acts 17:29
[3] 1 Cor 1:21

While it is true that we are able to seek and search after God and that God is not far from each one of us[2], yet he is not to be found by human wisdom.[3] If God could be discovered by human wisdom, we might be tempted to boast before the Lord. God, in his wisdom, chooses not be known by the wisdom of man.

However, the wisdom of modern man rarely appears in the form of rationalism these days. We now regard the rational, deductive process as tautological. The 'inductive' process based on empiricism is now much more in vogue. One wonders if God cares much about the distinction. He is not to be found by any human wisdom, be it empirical wisdom or rationalism. God can be seen through what he has created, because he has **chosen** to reveal himself in this way. It is not because we have devised a clever empirical method of testing and examination. The pursuit of signs and wonders to demonstrate the existence of God is a vain and futile exercise. God does not choose to reveal himself in miracles, but through the death of Jesus.

God, being personal, **chooses to reveal himself as he wills.** We can only know a person when the spirit of that person makes

[4] 1 Cor 2:11

them known.[4] If God chooses to absent himself, or to remain silent, then he will be unknown to us. He could hide his truth from anyone. Jesus said: "I praise you, Father, Lord of heaven and earth, because you have hidden these things from the wise and learned, and revealed them to little children. Yes, Father, because this was your good pleasure. All things have been committed to me by my Father. No one knows the Son except the Father, and no one knows the Father except the Son and those to

[5] Matt 11:25-27

whom the Son chooses to reveal him".[5]

It is by the foolishness of the cross, the word of the gospel, that God chooses to make himself known to man. This prevents man from having anything of which he can boast, save the Lord. Thus God hid his plans from the rulers of this age so that they could freely do what they wished: crucify the Lord of glory.[1] Even the prophets who predicted the sufferings of the Messiah were not able to understand more than God cared to reveal.[2]

It is only by the work of the Spirit of God in our lives, that we can see and understand the truth. God makes his "light shine in our hearts to give us the light of the knowledge of the glory of God in the face of Christ".[3] God, by the anointing of his Holy Spirit, teaches us about all things so that we do not need anyone to teach us.[4] Jesus promised the Spirit to lead his disciples into all truth, to remind them of the things they had seen and heard, and to convict the world of guilt in regard to sin and righteousness and judgement.[5]

Consequently, our knowledge of God comes from a prayerful obedience to the word of God revealed to us in the Scriptures. The Scriptures are full of this idea. God esteems the man of contrite heart, who trembles before his word.[6] It is this fear of the Lord which is the beginning of wisdom.[7] Obedience to the word of God saves us from foolishness and self-deception.[8] The word of God can make us wise for salvation in Christ Jesus and equip us for every good work.[9] It stands forever and is active and living and at work in our lives.[10] When we deal with the word of God, we deal with God himself.[11]

Thus God is sovereign in revelation.

[1] 1 Cor 1:18-2:16

[2] 1 Peter 1:10-12

[3] 2 Cor 4:6

[4] 1 John 2:27

[5] John 14-16
[6] Isa 66:2
[7] Psalm 111:10
[8] James 1:22

[9] 2 Tim 3:15-17
[10] 2 Tim 3:15-17; Heb 4:12-13; 1 Thess 2:13; 1 Pet 1:22-25

[11] Heb 4:12f;3:7 cf 4:7

God is sovereign in redemption

God's sovereignty is not limited by man's wilfulness. The sinfulness of man was, and is, his own choice. But the choices of men are not outside God's plans, nor can they ever thwart them. This sovereignty of God over the wills of men is seen most clearly in the death of Jesus. From before the foundation of the world, Christ was chosen to be the means of redemption.[12] Wicked men put him to death by nailing him to the cross and yet he was handed over by God's set purpose and foreknowledge.[13] Though men might have thought that they were rejecting God and thwarting his plans,[14] at the same time they were in fact fulfilling his plans. There is **dual authorship** for the action, a dual authorship that has different responsibility because of the different motivation behind it. It was the purpose of God that Christ should die for the salvation of mankind. It was the purpose of men to crucify Christ, that they may have done with

[12] 1 Peter 1:18-20

[13] Acts 2:23

[14] cf 1 Cor 2:8-9

him. God's sovereign plan used man's wilfulness to bring about God's purposes.

This kind of dual authorship, which demonstrates God's sovereign power over man, is seen often in the history of the Scriptures. In Genesis 50:20 we find that the action of Joseph's brothers was meant for evil, but that God meant it for good. In Proverbs 21:1, we find that the king's heart is in the hand of the Lord who turns it and directs it wherever he pleases. Or in 2 Corinthians 8:16,17, we are told that Titus is going to the Corinthians because God has put in his heart a concern for them, and because he has accepted an appeal from Paul to go to them, and because he is travelling on his own initiative!

This sovereign control of God over the affairs of mankind underpins the redemption of the world. From the first reference to the gospel in Genesis 3:15, to the calling of Abraham, to the sending of the people into Egypt and their rescue under Moses, to the establishment of the Kingdom under David and Solomon and the destruction of the Kingdom in Babylon—all is under the control of God.

A good case study is found in Isaiah 45 where Cyrus the Persian king is called the Lord's 'anointed', that is, his Christ. God has raised him up to subdue nations, and he promises to go before Cyrus to level the mountains and break down the gates in conquest. All this is done for the sake of Israel, that they might be rescued out of Babylon. Cyrus is God's instrument, even though he does not acknowledge God or know him.

Man, being sinful, does not seek the redemption of God. We have all turned our backs on God and run away from him. But God, being the sovereign Lord of redemption, has taken the initiative to chase after us. From the moment of the fall he revealed his plan to crush Satan's head under the foot of the woman's offspring.[1] He chose Abraham and Israel and David to establish his covenants. He had, even before the fall, chosen to send his Son into the world, to redeem it.[2] He organised the whole history of Israel to provide a meaningful context in which Jesus could die for the sins of the world. Through the death and resurrection of his Son, he has poured out his Spirit into the world to bring the forgiveness of sins through the preaching of the gospel of the cross.

[1] Gen 3:15

[2] 1 Pet 1:18-20; Eph 1:4-10

1. Response to the Gospel

Even though we are responsible for repentance and faith, God is still sovereign in our response to the gospel. Our faith comes to us by God's ordination, just as our repentance is given to us by his Spirit. Note how the conversion of a group of Gentiles is described in Acts: "When the Gentiles heard this they were glad and honoured the word of the Lord; and all who were appointed for eternal life believed."[1] And the response of the Jewish Christians? "When they heard this, they had no further objections and praised God, saying, 'So then, God has granted even the Gentiles repentance unto life'."[2] It is God who begins the good work in us, just as it is God who will bring it to completion.[3] God grants us not only to believe, but also to suffer for Christ.[4] From beginning to end, our salvation is by the grace of God—the gift of God—so that we cannot boast, not even of our faith and repentance.[5] The invitation is open to all to come and believe in the Son, and all who come will be saved—yet only those whom the Father draws who will come.[6] The Thessalonians believed that the word preached by Paul was really the word of God and Paul thanks **God** that they had such a spiritual discernment.[7]

[1] Acts 13:48

[2] Acts 11:18

[3] Phil 1:6
[4] Phil 1:29

[5] Eph 2:8f;
1Cor 1:26-2:5
[6] John 6:35-37, 43-45

[7] 1Thess 2:13

The same working of the sovereignty of God through the wills of men is seen in our sanctification and perseverance to the judgement day. We are called upon to continue in the faith, to stand firm to the end, to work out our salvation with fear and trembling. Yet it is God who is at work in us to will and to act according to his good purpose.[8] It is he who will sanctify us and keep us blameless until the coming of our Lord Jesus Christ.[9] Jude 21 instructs us to **keep ourselves in God's love**. But in Jude 1, we are addressed as those who are **kept by Jesus Christ** and in Jude 24 we read of **him who is able to keep us from falling** and to present us before his glorious presence without fault and with great joy.

2. Sanctification and perseverance

[8] Phil 2:12f
[9] 1 Thess 5:23-24

Many people deny the sovereignty of God in redemption. Most seek to establish some place for **our** contribution to the process. Frequently they argue that we need to contribute works in addition to the death of Jesus. Sometimes these are the works of the law; more often they are the works of religious ritual. Sometimes these works are limited to our free will or choice— we are saved by the death of Jesus **plus** our decision to repent.

Often God is viewed as desperately trying to win a battle with man's sinfulness, unable to get us back to the Garden. The history of Israel is seen as a kind of religious saga, with repeated episodes of God setting the people right, then falling asleep while they rebelled against him. Finally, when all else fails, God sends his Son—an afterthought, a contingency plan. God, it is said, would love everybody to enjoy health and prosperity and faith, but is unable to bring it about in the lives of people who rebel against him. When bad things happen to Christians

3. Objections

particularly, it is because of God's impotence. He is stymied by our lack of godliness, standing on the sideline lamenting his inability to act.

The Bible screams out against this view of an impotent God. God creates both prosperity and adversity, both wealth and woe.[1] He sends sickness, destruction and judgement upon people.[2] He has subjected the whole creation to futility and decay.[3] Satan never acts without bringing about God's purposes, even though he is in direct opposition to God. God's plans are never hindered by man's sinfulness nor dependent upon man's godliness. God is truly the sovereign Lord in redemption.

[1] Isa 45:7
[2] Lamentations 3:38
[3] Romans 8:1ff

God is sovereign in final judgement

God's final purposes will not be found in this world. He has planned a day upon which he will judge the world in righteousness. On that day, this world will be done away with and a new heaven and new earth created in which righteousness will dwell. God is not slow in fulfilling this promise, though he is staying his hand to give ample opportunity for men to repent. But as surely as his word created the world and then later destroyed it by the flood, so he has declared his intention to judge the world in his good time.[4]

[4] 2 Peter 3

The world will not be destroyed by mankind. It is God who will destroy this world, not any 'accident'. This final destruction will be carried out in justice and mercy—all will appear before the judgement seat of God.

In God's good time (a time not known to us, for God in his sovereignty has chosen not to reveal it[5]) he will reveal his Son in his glorious resurrection. At that time we will receive our resurrection bodies and be adopted as God's sons, changed into the glorious likeness of his Son.[6]

[5] Mark 13:32

[6] Phil 3:20f; Rom 8:28-30; Col 3:1-4; 1John 3:1-3

At present, God is placing all things under the feet of his risen Son and the last enemy to be defeated will be death itself. When everything is under Christ's feet, he will hand the Kingdom over to his Father so that he may be all in all.[7] In the present, it is appointed for every man to die once and then to face judgement.[8] Those who have already died will not miss out on the return of the Lord. But the day of God will be sudden and unexpected like a thief in the night.[9] Eventually we must all stand before the judgement seat of God[10] and the judgement seat of Christ.[11] The Father has given all judgement into the hands of the Son.[12]

[7] 1 Cor 15:24-28

[8] Heb 9:27

[9] 1 Thess 4:13-5:10
[10] Rom 14:9-12
[11] 2 Cor 5:10
[12] John 5:22,27; 17:31

Thus in every aspect of judgement, it is the sovereign Lord with whom we must deal.

Responding to God's sovereignty

The fear of the Lord is the beginning of wisdom. A God who is less than sovereign is not to be feared. A God who is sovereign is one in whom we should stand in awe, tinged with fright. His sovereign love in redemption will enable us to call him Father. But his might in creation and judgement and the wonder of his revelation to us, should lead us to tremble at his word, contrite in spirit. Such a person, who fears the Lord, is esteemed by him.

Think it through

1   Work out how you might explain the 'dual authorship' of our redemption to a young Christian.

2   Why do we often find the doctrine of God's sovereignty difficult or objectionable?

The Basis

The Doctrinal Basis of the Australian Fellowship of Evangelical Students (AFES), on which this training programme is based, is used throughout Australia as the doctrinal standard of Evangelical student groups. It reads as follows:

A   The divine inspiration and infallibility of Holy Scripture, as originally given, and its supreme authority in all matters of faith and conduct.

B   The unity of the Father, the Son and the Holy Spirit in the Godhead.

C   The universal sinfulness and guilt of human nature since the fall, rendering man subject to God's wrath and condemnation.

D   The conception of Jesus Christ by the Holy Spirit and his birth of the virgin Mary.

E   Redemption from the guilt, penalty and power of sin, only through the sacrificial death, as our representative and substitute, of jesus Christ, the incarnate Son of God.

F   The bodily resurrection of Jesus Christ from the dead.

G   The necessity of the work of the Holy Spirit to make the death of Christ effective in the individual sinner, granting him repentance toward God and faith in Jesus Christ.

H   The indwelling and work of the Holy Spirit in the believer.

I   The expectation of the personal return of the Lord Jesus Christ.